MISS BRENDA and the Loveladies

Miss Brenda *and the* Loveladies

One woman's brush with prison...
A comminity of women fighting the odds for survival on the outside...

A Heartwarming True Story of Grace, God, and Gumption

BRENDA SPAHN

and

IRENE ZUTELL

WATERBROOK
PRESS

Miss Brenda and the Loveladies
Published by WaterBrook Press
12265 Oracle Boulevard, Suite 200
Colorado Springs, CO 80291

Some names in this book have been changed to protect the identities of the persons involved.

Trade Paperback ISBN 978-0-307-73219-4
Hardcover ISBN 978-0-307-73217-0
eBook ISBN 978-0-307-73218-7

Cover design by Mark D. Ford

Published in the United States by WaterBrook Multnomah, an imprint of the Crown Publishing Group, a division of Penguin Random House LLC, New York.

The Library of Congress cataloged the hardcover edition as follows:
Spahn, Brenda.
Miss Brenda and the loveladies : a heartwarming true story of grace, God, and gumption / Brenda Spahn with Irene Zutell. — First Edition.
pages cm
ISBN 978-0-307-73217-0 — ISBN 978-0-307-73218-7 (electronic) 1. Church work with prisoners—United States. 2. Women prisoners—Religious life. 3. Women prisoners—Rehabilitation. 4. Spahn, Brenda. I. Title.
BV4340.S634 2014
259'.509761—dc23

2013034329

Printed in the United States of America
2015

10 9 8 7 6 5 4 3 2

Special Sales
Most WaterBrook Multnomah books are available at special quantity discounts when purchased in bulk by corporations, organizations, and special-interest groups. Custom imprinting or excerpting can also be done to fit special needs. For information, please e-mail SpecialMarkets@WaterBrookMultnomah.com or call 1-800-603-7051.

To my husband, Jeff Spahn, my children,
my twenty grandchildren, and my two great-grandchildren,
who have loved and supported me in who I am
rather than in who they wanted me to be.

To Jason, my wonderful stepson, my hero
behind the scenes, who is now with the Lord.

To all the women of the Lovelady Center—
those who are alive, and those who have died.

And to Don McGriff, who is now with the Lord,
and who was with us in the early days.

Contents

Introduction

Make sure you are doing what God
wants you to do—then do it
with all your strength.

GEORGE WASHINGTON

I was raised in a trailer. My parents struggled to feed and clothe me. Because I grew up without having much, I promised myself one day I'd be very rich.

Decades later, I had built a successful business. I finally had what I could only dream of as a child—a big house, fancy cars, expensive jewelry, and all the material things I could ever want.

At the height of success, I found myself under investigation for a crime I didn't commit. I faced the possibility of a lengthy prison sentence. All those possessions I had accumulated and cherished I was likely to lose. I had always felt I was in control of my life and my destiny. Once I was at the mercy of the legal system, I realized I was in control of nothing.

I lost my business, but I found another calling. I lost my riches, but I discovered riches of the spirit. I lost my faith in the system, but I discovered another faith—a faith in things that never depreciate or corrode or collapse. I found faith in God and the indomitable power of redemption—for myself and for a group of incarcerated women who'd been catastrophically abused by the system, by spouses, by parents, and by themselves.

Instead of chasing the American Dream, rehabilitating these women became my career. I learned that within each of them—even the most terrifyingly brutal felons—dwelled an undeniable spark of the divine.

Junkies, grifters, armed robbers, prostitutes, drunks, dealers, and murderers became my new social circle. They were former inmates of the Julia Tutwiler Prison for Women in Wetumpka, Alabama—another monolithic bureaucracy that warehoused the forgotten until they disappeared, returned, or died. Its motto could have been "Abandon hope."

They became the Loveladies. In the beginning, no name would have been more improbable. In time, no name could have been more fitting.

This is my story.

This is their story.

Meet the Loveladies.

1

Have I Lost My Mind?

Fear is faith that it won't work out.

ELBERT HUBBARD

"Oh my Lord, what have I done!" I gasped. I stared out the kitchen window as six violent criminals stomped up my driveway. Hunter, my four-year-old adopted son, stood on tiptoes trying to get a glimpse of what had me so terrified.

"Your mama has messed up big-time," I said.

For the last month, I had pictured this moment time and time again—but it had looked very different. In my imagination, the women would skip up the driveway, giggling and talking excitedly. I'd open the door with a loud "Welcome!" and women would race toward me, enveloping me in big, grateful bear hugs. After they'd thanked me profusely for being so wonderful, we'd sit around the kitchen table, have lunch, drink tea, share laughs, and get to know each other.

But these women stomping up my driveway didn't look like they wanted tea. They looked like they wanted blood.

Had I lost my mind?

Jeff, my husband, had predicted this. "You'll get yourself killed, Brenda," he said when I first told him my plan to rehabilitate female convicts. "You've had a lot of wild schemes in your life, but this is the craziest I've ever heard." Yes, but a lot of my schemes had worked out, and besides, this was different. This time it wasn't about me.

Now six very scary women, just released from the roughest women's prison in the country, were in my driveway.

I thought I had figured it all out. After spending months helping female convicts at a work release center, I thought I understood them. I had spoken with the inmates, we had prayed together, and they had seemed genuine in their desire to turn their lives around and start over.

But now I doubted everything. How could I have been so stubborn, so driven, so foolish? *How could I have put my little boy in danger?*

The night before, I'd combed through their "jackets"—prison files—and discovered with horror that the parole board wasn't sending me the nonviolent offenders I'd visited at the work release center. Instead, the women who had just shown up in front of my house had spent, collectively, one hundred years behind bars for crimes such as armed robbery, possession, drug dealing, prostitution, and manslaughter. I found out later that these were the hopeless cases—cases stamped CANNOT BE REHABILITATED—that all other programs had rejected.

At the work release center, I helped women who were struggling to get their lives together. But the women coming to my home were so hardened, so dangerous, that the system had given up on them. These were not the women I had bargained for.

I was supposed to rehabilitate them? *For the next nine months to a year?*

I wrapped my arms tight around Hunter. I should have dropped him off with the nanny, but I had been running late. My heart pounded so hard I was sure Hunter could hear it beating. I didn't want to scare him, so I took a breath and tried to find a portion of calm.

It wasn't that I hadn't prepared. I'd hired a housemother, a cook, and a driver. I owned a six-thousand-square-foot house with seven bedrooms and six bathrooms on ten acres of property that no one lived in. Hob Hill was perfect: it would become my "whole-way" house for parolees as they transitioned into the real world.

This is a good plan, I reassured myself.

These women would learn a skill and receive counseling, therapy, and, if need be, treatment for addiction. Since my program was faith-based, I'd teach them about Jesus, His unconditional love, the power of faith, and the reality of redemption. Then I'd get in my Cadillac Escalade and hightail it back to my new home in a gated community a few miles away.

I reminded myself that I was just supervising this program. You see, I'd be able to supervise it without really getting my hands dirty. I wouldn't give up my whole life. This would be more a hobby than a vocation.

And this is how I'll be able to keep that promise I made.

Much of my family had been understandably furious with me for pressing forward with my plan, but Melinda, my twenty-eight-year-old, caught my passion and crazy vision. She and I had spent the last month preparing for the women's arrival. I bought couches, chairs, and tables for the common areas and beds, comforters, dressers, and night tables for the seven bedrooms. I painted the rooms in calming colors—blues, yellows, and every shade of purple. Each bedroom was named after a fruit of the Spirit—joy, peace, self-control, love, patience, kindness, goodness—which I'd carefully painted on the bedroom doors. Each room had color-matching comforters and thick bath towels. I'd decorated the rooms with paintings—many of my favorite getaway, the beach—and supplied them with empty frames so the women could fill them with photographs of their children and families.

I put the word out to churches that I was looking to hire a cook, a driver, and, most important, a housemother who would run the program in my absence.

I soon found the perfect housemother—Claudia. She was forty-eight, single, big, and strong with a gruff, no-nonsense attitude. She had spent time volunteering at the work release center. When I met with her, she told me that God had called her into prison ministry and she was ready to get started.

I asked if the thought of working with female ex-cons frightened her. She laughed as if I'd asked the most insane question. "I'll take tigers by the tail," she said. "This is the work I was meant to do. I'm not afraid. It's my calling. I know I am going to change lives. The Lord sent me to do this."

I hired Claudia on the spot. She was so excited that she hired a moving company to haul all her bedroom and living room furniture into the upstairs master suite and office area. After she surveyed her new home, she nodded. "This is where I'm meant to be."

Likewise I'd hired a cook and a driver.

I could make this work. I *had* to make this work. For months I'd pleaded with the parole board to release women into my custody so I could help them get their lives back on track. I had told the board their system didn't work and needed an overhaul. After all, 30 percent of the women released from Alabama prisons returned to prison within the first six months.

They laughed at me. "What do you know about rehabilitating these women?"

"I know that giving them ten dollars and a bus ticket is just about the dumbest thing I've ever heard. I know I can do better."

In Alabama, there were only two options for newly released prisoners: They'd get their ten bucks and transportation back to where they committed their crimes. In a short time they'd go back to old ways with old friends. Or they'd spend a few weeks in a halfway house, where they'd receive food and shelter but little else, then be put back on the street.

No matter their destination—bus ticket home or halfway house—once they were released, these women had one thing in common: they had no hope. And they had no hope because they couldn't envision a future outside of prison.

To me, the solution was obvious. My whole-way house would be a place where they could change their lives by learning skills and receiving counseling. We would give them a picture of a future they themselves could create, one in which they could succeed.

I have always considered myself visionary, but the parole board used a different term—delusional. Ultimately I wore them down and they finally agreed, probably just to make me go away.

Now I realized they were trying to teach me a lesson. I was sure they were having a big laugh about it: *"I wonder if that crazy redhead is scared senseless yet. How long until she calls us to take them all back?"*

I crouched lower and squinted through the window, hoping the awnings outside shielded me from the women's view. My eyes landed on the scariest-looking woman I'd ever seen in my life. Was she even a woman? With a shaved head, baggy khakis, and an extra large navy-blue prison-issued polo shirt that covered her tanklike physique, she resembled a gangbanger looking for trouble. Her fists were clenched, and her eyes blazed with fury.

Why is she so angry? Doesn't she see how great her life is about to become?

The other women were right behind her. She was the gang leader and they were her loyal followers, standing so close to each other they appeared connected—an impenetrable wall about to storm my house. A heavyset woman who seemed devoid of the fury the rest possessed stopped to gawk at my home. Shaved Head snapped her face toward her and the woman's expression immediately turned grim.

Ken, the driver of the van who had shuttled the women from prison to my place, opened the back of the truck. The women collected their belongings. One by one, each woman pulled out a brown paper sack with her name written large in black marker. A paper sack! These were all their possessions in the whole world!

My heart sank. *What about clothes? shoes? things?* I hadn't realized they'd show up with next to nothing. In my naivety, I thought they'd spend most of today unpacking their belongings.

They were almost at the door—and I was paralyzed. Melinda, who hadn't been watching them through the window and had no idea what awaited her, realized I wasn't moving, so she headed to the door.

Dear Melinda, what have I gotten you into, and why are you so calm?

Of all the people in our family, Melinda was the one who had the most personal interest in my crazy dream. To be fair, my husband Jeff *couldn't* be there at Hob Hill—he needed to provide income for our family, and our real estate business was located more than four hours away in Gulf Shores. But Jeff, who'd been through plenty of "harebrained Brenda schemes" before, was admittedly not a fan of my "whole-way" idea, even as he tried to be supportive of me.

Melinda was the one who, ever since she'd been a little girl, had always been by my side. At eleven, she'd sit next to my desk and answer the phone as I filed clients' tax returns. When she was old enough, she worked with me. When I started helping women at the work release center, she had accompanied me. She was just as passionate as I was to help women turn their lives around.

I hadn't mentioned to Melinda that these women might be different from the work release darlings we'd worked with. Apprehensive as I had become from reading the files, I still held out hope that things would work out fine. But one glimpse of the crew of ex-cons who had just shown up shook me. Melinda had spent her life trusting me. Now she was an unwitting partner in my crazy scheme.

She opened the door wide.

I scooted toward her. "Welcome to my home," I blurted out, forcing a big smile.

The women glared at me. I waited for someone to say something. Instead, they pushed into the house, squeezing through the door in one massive pile. They forced themselves past me as if I wasn't even there.

I wanted to stop everything and yell out an order: *Get out of my house and get back in the van!* Maybe I could just give them some lunch and send them off, saying this was a big mistake.

Shaved Head came so close to me I could feel her breath on my face. I squeezed Hunter.

"I ain't gonna be no maid in a little white apron for you," she spat out, her voice growing louder with each word. "What the h***'s a g**d***** white woman gonna do with us? Lady, what kinda sh** do you think you're playing?"

Sharon "Shay" Curry. Even though she looked different from the photo in the prison jacket (she had hair back then), I recognized her. She was a forty-five-year-old black woman who'd been in and out of prison her whole life. She'd done it all—armed robbery, dealing and using drugs, prostitution, attempted murder.

Dear God, attempted murder!

Shay's nostrils flared and her eyes bore into me. I watched the other women study her. I could tell they were taking their cues from Shay. In the short time they'd been together—probably since the van ride over—Shay had become the unofficial ringleader.

I knew if I didn't win Shay over there would be no way to right this ship.

Where was Claudia? She'd been watching as the van pulled into my driveway, but I had no idea where she'd gone. It was her job to get the women settled into their rooms—not mine or Melinda's. Claudia, I told myself, would get the situation under control. She'd know how to handle Shay.

I took a deep breath, finally answering Shay, speaking as calmly as possible: "Well, I'm gonna help you get your life in order."

As soon as the words slipped out, I knew I'd made a mistake.

"You don't know sh** about me, lady," Shay hissed. "You're just some crazy white lady. How the h*** do you think you're gonna do that? What do you think you're going to do for me?"

My chest tightened and I felt dizzy. I scanned the room, searching for Claudia. The truth was, I didn't have any plans beyond getting these women into the house and introducing myself. In prison, every second of the day is scheduled. I had wanted to give the women a little breathing room. But already Shay was in my face, angrily demanding answers.

"What do you think you're gonna do, lady?"

I panicked and said just about the stupidest thing I could ever say: "I'm going to help you get your driver's license."

The women burst into laughter.

Shay looked like she'd just bit into something so vile she might be sick. "I've been driving my whole life, lady. I don't need no driver's license."

And then I said the second dumbest thing I could possibly say: "Well, how do you get insurance without a license?"

There was another fit of laughter. These women had thought they'd seen it all, but they'd never met a flaming-red-haired fifty-five-year-old woman like me before. I knew they had determined right then that I was a complete idiot.

I had an uprising on my hands. *Where will we hide if they get violent?*

I had to regain some kind of control before Shay took over my house.

"Oh, I forgot," I said, managing an edge of sarcasm. "You're all about breaking the law." I rolled my eyes. "You're real tough guys."

They stared at me, their mouths hanging open, shocked that I'd sassed Shay back. I was shocked too but couldn't help it—throughout my life my big mouth has gotten me into a lot of trouble. But occasionally it saves the day. I was praying that was the case now. Melinda shot me a look that said, *What are you thinking?* Then she turned toward the women and broke the ice. "Okay, ladies," she said, smiling sweetly, "how about I show y'all your rooms?"

The women followed Melinda down the hallway. Some gasped at the bedrooms I had decorated for them. After years of living in a cramped dorm with 160 other women, these rooms with one, two, or three beds or bunkbeds seemed to them like paradise. From the corner of my eye, I saw two of them claim one of the downstairs bedrooms. I watched them stifle giggles as they ran down the hall to fetch their paper bags of belongings.

Ken, the driver, was a director for alternative treatment programs at the University of Alabama at Birmingham (UAB). During the last few weeks he'd become an advocate, helping me prepare my house for the women. He must have thought I was doing fine because I had a big smile plastered on my face. Truth was, my smile was frozen. You've heard of people being scared silly? I was scared *smiling.*

He smiled back. "I'm taking off," he called out. "Is there anyone who wants to leave with me?" I heard some of the women giggling from the bedrooms.

"No!" one called out from a bedroom. "We're not going anywhere," others said. Shay stood silently in the hallway, her arms folded.

"What about you?" Ken asked Shay.

Go, I silently begged. *Tell him you want to leave. Now. I can handle these other women, but not you. Get your butt in that van. I never want to see you again.*

Shay scowled at Ken but didn't answer.

"Shay? You coming with me?"

Stop asking and just flippin' take her! I wanted to scream.

"Shay?"

There was a heavy silence. I could feel my future in that void. *If she leaves, I stand a chance. If she stays, I'm doomed to fail.*

"I'll stay," she said, as if she were doing us all a big favor.

And with that, Ken left me in a big house with five female ex-cons and one ringleader from hell.

Shay and the other women headed upstairs to check out the remaining bedrooms with Melinda. As soon as they disappeared, I heard the click of a door unlocking. Claudia ran out, stopping in her tracks when she saw me.

"Where have *you* been?" I asked. "I need you to help Melinda."

Claudia didn't move. Gone was the tough broad who was going to take the tigers by the tail. In her place was a timid woman whose eyes were filled with panic.

"I quit," she choked out.

I laughed. "You can't quit."

"I just did. And you should too. You're going to get yourself and your family killed."

Claudia couldn't do this to me. I had a plan—she would run the program, the cook would cook, the driver would drive, taking the women wherever they needed to go. And me? I'd check in once in a while and make sure they were all doing their jobs. "I'm not even going to be there," I told Jeff and my family when they expressed concern that I was putting myself in danger.

I tried to sound calm, but I was a wreck. My heart pounded, and I thought I might collapse. I steadied my voice: "You told me God called you to work with these women. He wouldn't just change His mind."

"The Lord might want me to work with prisoners, but not *these* prisoners! You're crazy. I want nothing to do with this insanity."

I opened my mouth to beg her to stay, but she swatted her hand in the air, turned, and ran off.

Just as she left, the cook and the driver came out from wherever they had been hiding. They too raced out the front door.

I stood in the living room, holding Hunter tight and paralyzed with all kinds of fear. I'd always had a plan, a next move. Now, for the first time I could remember, I had no idea what to do. I prayed for guidance. I prayed for answers. I prayed that these women wouldn't kill me.

Was God listening to any of my prayers? Or had He quit on me too?

2

Answered Prayer

It is not in the stars to hold our destiny
but in ourselves.

WILLIAM SHAKESPEARE

A few months before, I did not at all resemble that crazy do-gooder praying to God for answers. Well, crazy, yes. Do-gooder, no. Praying to God—not so much.

A few months before, I would never have allowed myself to be anywhere near a bunch of criminals. I certainly wouldn't have welcomed them into my home. If I had seen a woman like Shaved Head coming toward me, I would have jumped in my car, locked my doors, and sped away while dialing 911.

A few months before, I was Brenda Spahn, an entrepreneur, a world traveler, a shopaholic, and a self-indulgent brat who loved the finer things in life. I was in the business of making money. Not helping charity cases.

A few months before, I didn't know any convicts and had never seen the inside of a prison except on television shows.

A few months before, I believed if people were in prison, they deserved to be there.

But then, not long before, *I* nearly went to prison.

My story really begins on April 15, 2002, a beautiful spring day. Joy, a friend and employee, and I drove to my tax-preparation business near my home in Birmingham. Tax Max was our family business, with eighteen offices throughout the city. My sons Matthew and Beau, as well as Melinda's husband, Shawn, ran several of the offices, while Melinda worked with me in the main office. Miranda, my youngest daughter, was seventeen and still in high school, but I was sure she'd join us one day. We were a family who worked together and played together.

I was filled with excitement as I drove to the office. It was the last day of tax season. I couldn't wait to wrap up the season and unwind at the Island Princess, the name of my breathtaking beach house in Gulf Shores, a beautiful resort on the northern coast of the Gulf of Mexico.

But first I wanted to do what I did best—make more money. And it looked like the last day of tax season was going to be a great day for us. It was just a little after 6 a.m. and already the parking lot was filling up with cars.

I turned to Joy. "Can you flippin' believe this? It's going to be one crazy morning."

As soon as I spoke, people I assumed were clients jumped out of those cars and rushed toward us. A man yanked at the door of my Cadillac Escalade.

"I have a search warrant. This is a raid," he announced as if that explained everything.

Suddenly, the world became fuzzy. It was as if my brain had switched to a slower speed and the world was running at fast-forward around me. I realized these weren't clients but police officers and federal agents. But why were they at our business? Was there a burglary? An armed robbery? What was happening?

When I could finally speak, I said, "What's goin' on?"

The agent who had pulled the door open looked me hard in the eyes as if he were trying to see through me. He smirked. "You know."

"No, I do not know."

He didn't back off. "You know." His gaze seemed even more intense.

I got out of my car and ran toward the office.

The agent in charge followed me. "Unlock the door," he said. "I have a search warrant."

"What's this about?" I yelled. My hand was shaking so much that I couldn't fit the key into the lock. Mr. Agent-in-Charge yelled, "Break it down!" Another agent raced toward the door with a steel battering ram.

"No! Just give me a second," I pleaded.

I steadied my hand with my other hand and unlocked the door. As soon as it opened, agents rushed in and attacked the office, pulling open drawers and flinging files everywhere. My entire business soon littered the floor. Men wheeled out my possessions on dollies.

How can this be happening? Who do these people think they are? This was my life and they were treating it like it was trash.

"Why is this happening? Why are you here?"

"You know." It was that agent again—a six-foot-tall balding man with beady eyes and glasses. To me he looked like a weasel.

"I don't know."

"It seems you don't know much of anything," the weasel said smugly, adding that he was a criminal investigation agent with the Internal Revenue Service. "You're being investigated for fraud. You're looking at years in prison."

I was shocked and scared but mostly angry. The weasel seemed so certain of my guilt, so cocky in his accusations.

"This is complete insanity," I hissed.

The weasel shook his head. "You don't seem to understand the seriousness of this situation." Then he pulled out photos and laid them in front of me. He had pictures of me going into my house, going to the office, going to the grocery store. Now I was really scared. Why had he been following me?

Melinda arrived and was asked to speak to an agent in one of the offices. She was three months pregnant and battling morning sickness. As I peeked in on my daughter's meeting, I saw her body convulse in sobs.

Over the years, we'd all joked with Melinda that she was the Goody

Two-Shoes of the family. As a child, she never ever got into trouble. She was the student teachers always labeled "class role model." As a teenager, she never drank or smoked or did drugs. I don't remember her ever cussing. She was a mother's dream daughter. And now she was being treated like a criminal? I was furious. And when I get furious, watch out—even *I* don't know what's going to come out of my mouth.

I turned toward the weasel. "You must be the most dimwitted person I have ever known," I said, "because you're not going to find anything, Scooby Doo."

I called him Scooby Doo, the name of the cartoon canine amateur sleuth, because this investigation seemed so amateurish, so without merit. To me, filing taxes was as natural as breathing. I was raised on it and it had been my lifeblood during tough times. As a child, I learned the business from my mom, an accountant. As a teenager, I worked with her out of our tiny two-bedroom home in Birmingham. For a few years, I had even worked for the local Internal Revenue office. After I had my babies, I started filing taxes on the dining room table as a way to help support our growing family.

Over the years, I dipped my hands in other businesses—some succeeded and some failed miserably—but I always fell back on my tax-preparation skills. As my kids got older, I focused on the business and it flourished. Like my mother, I taught my children the ropes. We built an empire—one of the largest independently owned tax businesses in the state.

In the thirty-plus years that I'd been filing returns, I'd always tried hard to file honest tax returns while doing what was best for the client. I considered myself meticulous. I had a good reputation in the community. Surely this was a misunderstanding.

I believed any minute someone would barge into the room and say, "Sorry. This is a big mistake."

I kept waiting and waiting for that to happen. But it never did. I finally gave up and walked out of my office.

Outside, I was swarmed by television cameras and newspaper reporters. The IRS had called all the local media. We became the tax-day story—a cautionary tale of what happens if you cheat the government. In the eyes of the government and the media, we were already guilty.

Much, much later on I discovered that a former client had been accused of embezzling over $300,000 from a former employer. She had been told of a whistleblower law that stated if she turned someone in, her sentence would be reduced. So she turned us in.

To this day, I'm not sure why she chose us. But once she did, the system worked against us. The IRS operates within such a labyrinth of regulations that, if it wants to, it can find something to charge anyone with.

The agents analyzed more than eight thousand tax returns and discovered just eight that could be questioned as possible instances of tax evasion.

Poor Melinda became the focus of their investigation. It seems a few months earlier the IRS had sent to our business an undercover agent posing as the owner of a landscaping company. Melinda had handled his taxes. He wasn't satisfied with her work and pressed her to find loopholes so he could report less income and pay lower taxes. She admitted she had cut some corners.

"This is my fault. I made a mistake," she said over and over. "I've ruined the family business."

Melinda was pregnant with her third child, and she couldn't eat or sleep. She couldn't stop crying. We became deeply worried for her and her baby. We told her it wasn't her fault—she had filed so many perfect tax returns over the course of many years. We had been so swamped, so overworked—it could easily have happened to any of us, we said.

Meanwhile, I was accused of failing to provide adequate supervision.

Looking back, yes, we should have been more careful, more meticulous. I should have supervised my employees better. I suppose we were guilty of getting too big too fast and making some sloppy mistakes.

Even so, our occasional sloppiness should never have been used to create the mess this had become. I always had great faith in our justice system. Now I was getting a crash course in how easy it was for that same system to conspire against us.

As the days progressed, the situation became more and more dire. Melinda and I, as well as all the other children and spouses, were fingerprinted and our bank accounts were frozen. We were actually facing a real possibility of being sent to prison.

My attorney, David Cromwell Johnson, was considered to be the best criminal lawyer in Birmingham, maybe all of Alabama. He was very aggressive. Naturally, we formed an instant connection.

Small in stature, David was a voracious reader of anything war-related. He compared himself to a five-star general. He also compared himself to the champion horse Seabiscuit, who was also small, but who became a symbol of hope during the Great Depression.

"We'll fight 'em and never go down. I'm Seabiscuit, the fastest horse that ever lived. I just don't lose, Brenda."

I believed him. For the first time since the ordeal began, I felt hopeful. With David on our team, we couldn't fail.

Months later, David died in his sleep of a heart attack. He was only sixty-one. He was so well-known, it seemed all of Alabama was in mourning, but his death hit me hard because so much of my personal future depended on his defending me. I was completely devastated.

Things became grim again.

Sam, Melinda's lawyer, stepped in to defend me. He didn't have the same fighting spirit as David. Actually, he and Melinda didn't want to fight at all.

"I can't do this," she said, crying. "I made a mistake. I did something illegal. I didn't realize it was illegal, but I don't think that matters. I want to plead out. You and I both know that if it comes to a trial, I could never handle it. It's not in me. This is killing me."

My beautiful daughter. Her deep-blue eyes were so full of pain. It stabbed my heart. I knew I was responsible. I had brought her into the business, then pushed her and everyone else around me because I was obsessed with making as much money as possible. No one could move at my pace. I was too demanding. Too relentless.

"I just want this to be over," Melinda said. "It feels that no matter what we do, they will win. They will keep burying us. I don't want to go to jail. I couldn't handle it."

Jeff and the rest of my family disagreed with Melinda. "Of course you have to fight this," Jeff said.

Fighting was second nature to me. I thought about all of our hard work, all the money we had accumulated, all the things we had bought with our success—I had a mink coat and five closets jammed with clothes. We owned a beautiful home in Birmingham and several rental houses at the beach. I reflected on the joy I felt as the business blossomed. I remembered my childhood vow never to be poor again.

Yes, I had fought hard for all of what I now had. I wasn't about to let it be taken away from me.

Sometimes in life we make decisions that change the course of our destiny. I made mine one day later.

We were at the federal courthouse meeting with an officer to fill out paperwork. She asked us questions and typed our answers onto forms. I answered everything in my most intimidating voice.

The officer asked Melinda her address. We waited. And waited. Finally Melinda reached down and pulled her driver's license from her wallet and read her address from the license. She was so upset she couldn't remember where she lived.

Something ached in me. When I looked at Melinda, I didn't see a nearly thirty-year-old woman; I saw the baby I'd held in my arms just yesterday.

I thought about Melinda's children. Who would raise them if she was sent to prison? I thought of my adopted son, Hunter, who needed me to be there for him. I thought of my husband, who had endured so much humiliation and watched our bank account dwindle as we paid exorbitant attorney fees.

So I made a decision.

I told Sam, "Do what you need to do. I'll plead guilty to stop this nonsense."

By pleading guilty to preparation of four false tax returns, we'd most likely avoid jail. It would cost us nearly everything else, but I was ready to move on. I didn't want the threat of prison hanging over Melinda or me.

We were told that as part of the agreement, we'd most likely be fined, and Melinda and I would be unable to prepare tax returns for a period of time. That was fine with me—I had already sworn that I would never prepare another tax return as long as I lived. It was also communicated to us that the judge still might try to set an example with us. It was possible we'd receive a small jail sentence. There were no guarantees.

Our lawyer said he'd call me back with the judge's decision.

Later that day, I was alone in my office. I didn't feel the relief I'd expected. Instead, I felt panic. After all that, would we still serve prison time?

Exhausted, I put my head on my desk. How could I have let this happen to our business? My family? Melinda blamed herself, but I was really the one who was at fault. During the tax season we'd worked all day and sometimes through the night, seven days a week—and she had been newly pregnant and sick much of the time. In my unrelenting quest for money, I had become a ruthless boss, even with my own family. Yet I thought the rewards were worth it all.

There in the quiet of my office, I realized this wasn't really true. I had all the material possessions I could ever want, but I wasn't happy. I didn't feel fulfilled. Ever since I was a little girl, I felt I was supposed to do something more with my life. I felt I had a greater purpose. But what? I didn't know. I prayed for God to show me the way.

But He didn't answer me.

Or so I thought.

Maybe I just wasn't listening.

Instead, I had tried to fill the void within me by making and spending money. I had tried to buy peace of mind as if it were on a hanger at Saks.

Was God telling me it was time to stop ignoring Him and start listening to His call, the call of my destiny?

In those moments, the frenzy that had consumed my life suddenly seemed miles away. My heart became quiet. I knew the answer.

I closed my eyes and prayed. And I prayed with a vengeance: *Okay, Lord, You know what? I'll walk away from everything. I'll do anything and everything You want me to do. I'll stop focusing on money and start focusing on doing Your work. Help me. I'll change my ways. Just please don't make me go to prison.*

I guess I should call my prayer more of a negotiation.

When I opened my eyes, I felt calm for the first time in months, maybe years. When had I stopped praying like that? It used to be something I had done all the time. Even my parents at one point renewed their faith when they saw how serious I was about mine. When had all that gone out of my life?

I looked at the stack of papers on my desk. On the top was a form for an ordination class that had come in the mail. I'd always been interested in the ministry. When I was a child, it had felt like a calling. When the church was empty, I'd lock the doors and preach to my friends. But when I became an adult, I'd been too practical, too concerned about money to make the time.

I'd kept the form as a reminder of the person I had once thought I'd become. I had told myself that one day, when things slowed down, when I made enough money, when I bought enough things, I'd fill out the form. But I knew all along I had been lying to myself. I had no intention of ever having enough.

Now it made perfect sense. Almost without thinking, I filled out the form, scanned it into the computer, and hit send.

Just a few minutes later the phone rang. My attorney. "We struck a deal. You and Melinda won't have to go to prison." Under the deal, we would each pay a small fine and wear an ankle bracelet as part of our six-month in-house probation. "But it's over," he said, "and you can get back to your life."

Back to my life?

After eighteen months, the ordeal was finally over. Had it been a coincidence that the phone rang right after I'd prayed and signed that document? Part of me wanted to chalk it up to that, to forget about my promise, to get back to my old life. But in my heart I knew it was no coincidence.

The IRS raid was a wake-up call from God. This was not the time to go back. I would make changes.

But what would they be?

I closed my eyes, prayed, and listened. I heard the answer—and it wasn't what I expected. It wasn't what I wanted to hear. It was terrifying, yet so obvious.

In fact, it was perfect.

I would minister to a group of people I myself could easily have joined—if fate had taken a different turn, if God hadn't answered my prayers.

I'd minister to women prisoners.

3

Chocolate-Covered Strawberries

Faith is taking the first step even when
you don't see the whole staircase.

MARTIN LUTHER KING JR.

I didn't know how to begin. I didn't know who to call or what to do. I didn't even know the names of the women's prisons in Alabama. When I asked around, George, a minister friend, told me about a 340-bed work release center for women in Birmingham.

I had never heard of a work release center. George explained that it housed inmates who were permitted to hold jobs outside of prison. I decided if these women were allowed to mingle with the general population, they couldn't be too scary.

So I figured that's where I'd start my ministry.

George agreed to drive me over so I could get a look. As we cruised past the center, I told George to stop the car so I could go in and introduce myself.

George laughed. "You can't just go in. You have to make an appointment. Call them later today and set something up."

"Oh, come on! Just stop the dang car and let me run in there and talk to the warden."

"You don't just run into a prison and talk to the warden," George said, laughing.

"Why the heck not?"

"Because it doesn't work that way."

I narrowed my eyes, letting him know I wasn't messing around. "I've put this on hold long enough."

Exasperated, George sighed and stopped the car. "Okay. Go ahead and try."

I walked to the door and pushed. It was stuck, so I pushed harder. I turned back toward George, who had an amused look on his face.

"See, it's not even locked," I yelled as I pushed the door with my whole body.

The door finally swung open. Immediately an alarm shrilled. I tripped over a display of potted plants that had been lined against the door on the inside. Suddenly, I was surrounded by office workers and prison officers.

Someone yelled, "How'd you get in here?"

"How do you think? I opened the door."

"That door has been locked for years. The entrance is on the side of the building, not here. This is never opened."

"I'm telling you, I just opened it."

"Impossible."

I was standing knee-deep in plants. One of the plants had tipped over, and dirt covered the dingy linoleum floor. *How do I get into these messes?* I stepped over the dirt and cleared my throat.

"Could someone take me to see the warden?"

I was taken to Captain Patricia Hood, the interim warden, who had already heard about my unconventional entrance and didn't seem too pleased to see me. A tall, thin, meticulously dressed black woman, Captain Hood seemed very serious, very businesslike, and very much not in the mood to deal with some curly haired, redheaded clown who had barged into the place.

Without introducing herself or asking who I was, she asked, "Why are you here?"

"Well, ma'am, I believe the Lord is calling me to work with these women. I don't know a thing about them. I've never been in a prison in my life, and I haven't been to a jail. The closest I came to breaking the law was sneaking into a drive-in movie in the trunk of a car when I was sixteen and—"

"So you're telling me you want to preach?"

"Yes ma'am, I do."

"Well, you'll have to fill out paperwork," she said.

"Fine."

"It could take a while before you hear from us."

"How long?

"Maybe up to six months."

"*Six months?* I'm here now. I'm ready to preach and teach," I said.

Secretly I was deeply relieved. Maybe this was a sign from God that I wasn't supposed to do this. Maybe He was letting me off the hook. I had to make the effort—I'd promised God. It was our bargain. So I was here. I had tried. But if He wasn't taking me up on it... I could barely stifle an enormous grin. Clearly Captain Hood didn't take me seriously. She thought I wasn't prison material, and she was trying to let me down easy. I was fine with that.

Still, I made one last try: "Well, okay, but I think this is what the Lord wants me to do."

With that I left her office. I practically skipped down the hallway, feeling very free. If God had really meant for me to preach to women prisoners, I wouldn't have been met with such clear resistance. Amen!

Then I stopped in my tracks as disappointment enveloped me. If this wasn't what I was supposed to do, then what? Had I been wrong? Had I imagined this calling?

Am I crazy?

Dear Lord, what do You want me to do?

Just as I grabbed the handle of the front door, a guard raced toward me.

What did I do this time?

"Captain Hood wants to see you for a minute."

I returned to her office, wondering what this was about. *Does she want me to pay for the damage to those plants?*

Captain Hood stared at me, silent for a moment, as if trying to figure me out. Then she smiled and said, "Be here tomorrow night at seven."

When I arrived the next night, it seemed that news of my entrance the day before had traveled among the staff. Everyone knew me. I was the woman who forced opened locked doors, knocked over plants, set off alarms, and barged in to see the warden—the crazy redhead who had actually broken *into* prison.

"I'm here," I said to one of the officers. "What do I do now?"

The officer smirked. "What do you wanna do, Miss *Span*?" I opened my mouth to correct his mispronunciation of my name, but stopped myself.

"Heck, I don't know. I guess I want to tour the place or something."

The officer laughed. "Well, okay, Miss *Span,* we're gonna let you go in and meet the women."

I thought someone would come with me, but the officer unlocked the heavy prison door and waved me on. I've since learned that nobody ever tours prisons or work release centers without being chaperoned. I have no idea why they let me go off on my own. I imagine I was sort of a novelty for them.

Most of the ministers who come to prisons are serious, no-nonsense people. Here I was—a loud, brazen woman who barged in to clearly unchartered territory. They were enjoying the entertainment, the show. They wanted to see what would happen next. When would the redhead start running down the hall begging to get out?

I forced a smile as I walked down the dreary, fluorescent-lit hallway, nodding to anyone who passed me. The air was filled with a stomach-turning stench, so I pinched my nose shut. I peeked in one of the three dorm rooms and saw the reason for the horrible odor—the room had a few microwaves, and women stood next to them heating dinners.

I studied one woman as she picked up a ketchup bottle. "What's your problem?" the woman snarled.

"Hey there, my name's Brenda and I just want to meet some of you guys. I'm a Christian, and I want to talk to you about Jesus. Stuff like that."

She turned away and squeezed ketchup over a plate of ramen noodles. "We have church services already."

I moved closer and smiled. "Well, you know what? I don't really like church services like that too much. Do you? If some of those people came in here and tried to talk to me about Jesus, I probably would be mad and wouldn't listen."

She paused, turned toward me, and slowly nodded her head. A few of the woman near her stopped what they were doing to listen.

"Yeah. You're right."

"Trust me, I'm just like you. I've been in trouble. I've done a lot of things in my life that I'm not proud of. I'm a little bit different from other ministers."

They looked at me, their mouths hanging open. "Are you really a minister?"

I laughed. "Barely."

"Really?" They laughed.

"I only got ordained so it would be easier to get in and see you."

They laughed. "You'd go through all that trouble to come to this dump?"

The woman who had been making noodles held out a plate for me.

"Have some. It's spaghetti."

I forced myself to take a taste. I smiled and told her it was wonderful.

It was one of the most disgusting things I have ever eaten. Ketchup on noodles? I have a weak stomach as it is, so I tried my hardest not to gag. With my plastic fork I moved the noodles around my plate, then back again, hoping nobody would notice I wasn't really eating.

I told the women I'd be back the next night. "I'll pray with some of you. It will probably be a little different than what you are used to. But you'll really enjoy it, I promise. Maybe we will have a short service too. Since I don't know a thing about preaching, I'll just be talking. Bring your friends because I'll feel really bad if no one shows up."

The next night I returned with Melinda. I was put in a small, drab white room with nothing in it but a metal table and four chairs. A few women were waiting outside the door.

"Hey, if you wanna pray, just come on in," I yelled so anyone could hear me all the way down the hall.

I had them come in one by one, and I prayed with each woman privately.

When I pray, I talk. I know many pray in a formal language, speak with words like *thou* and *art* and overcomplicate the sentences so no one really understands what is being said. I just pray to God as if I am talking to a good friend. (He is my best friend, so it works out well for me.)

I told the women that just because they messed up, that didn't mean God had abandoned them. God was always there, waiting for them. All they had to do was talk to Him. "I'm sure you've been running from the Lord, but you don't have to anymore," I said. "He's always here for you."

After I'd prayed with a few women, Melinda, who was waiting by the door, whispered to me, "Go faster."

I gave her an annoyed look. Didn't she understand that these women needed time and attention, not fast-food prayer?

Halfway through my next prayer, Melinda stuck her head inside and interrupted. "Hurry!"

I was getting more and more irritated. I went over to her to set her straight: "What are you doing? You keep interrupting me and it's very annoying. I can't pray any faster!"

"Well, you better try. Look out the door, Mother."

She turned toward the hallway. I followed her gaze and couldn't believe what I saw.

A long line of female convicts snaked all the way down the hall and around the corner. Apparently the word had quickly spread. Here was a minister who didn't judge them, didn't lecture them, and talked to God using real words.

Here was someone talking about a God who really cared.

"You must be doing something right," Captain Hood told me when it was time to leave. "Usually a minister is lucky if five or six women come to pray."

On my next visit, the warden had decided to move me into a larger room. When I arrived, there were sixty women crammed in, waiting for me. Prison workers shook their heads.

"This has never happened for as long as I've been here, Miss *Span,*" one told me.

I realized they expected me to preach. I had no idea what to say. I had enjoyed praying with each woman, but I didn't like the idea of holding a service. I'd been a motivational speaker on occasion and wasn't afraid of standing up in front of a crowd. But I thought of myself more as a minister to individuals than a preacher to a congregation. I could tell by the way the women were looking at me that they expected me to say something powerful. But I had nothing prepared, and nothing was coming to mind.

What can I say that will touch them?

I remembered what some women had told me the last time I was there. What had separated me from other ministers was that I had listened to them rather than preached at them. That's what I needed to do now. "We're going to do something different today," I said to them. "I'm going to ask you to give me a praise report."

"A *what*?"

"We always have to give God praise for the small stuff He does for us. He's not going to give us the big stuff if we don't thank Him for the small stuff. So I want you to tell me something good that happened to you during the last week."

I know that asking prisoners to tell what they're thankful for might sound like a truly insane idea. However, I believe that every day everyone—even an incarcerated woman—has a moment that helps her rise above her situation, a moment she can be thankful for, a moment in which she can feel God's presence in her life.

My incarcerated congregation seemed to understand this too. They were quiet, but thinking.

No one said a word.

"Come on," I prompted. "Tell me something wonderful that's happened to you in the last few days."

Some started calling out. One mentioned visits from children. Others spoke of seeing husbands, parents. One mentioned that she was close to her EOS.

"EOS?"

"End of sentence," I was told in unison.

Then, from the back of the room, a small voice called out, "Chocolate-covered strawberries."

Some women started nodding excitedly. All at once, different voices told the story of the wonderful strawberries a visitor had brought to the center earlier in the week.

"It was the most amazing thing I've eaten," one said. "I can't stop thinking about how good that strawberry was."

I smiled. Inwardly I was deeply moved. A gift like that wouldn't have meant anything to me. Actually, I probably would have taken the whole box and without a second thought just passed it off to a coworker. I certainly wouldn't have been thankful for it.

Here these women tasted a single strawberry, and it had made their week. I tried my best not to cry, but I felt a tear run down my face.

What type of life do you have when a single chocolate-covered strawberry is the highlight of your week?

The next time I went to the center, I was determined to experience life from their perspective.

"Where's your bathroom?" I asked one of the women.

"Right inside the dorm, but you don't want to use it. Go to the one in the front, by the offices."

"No, I want to use yours," I said.

The woman looked at me like I was out of my mind. "Trust me, you do not. Go to the nice one in the front."

I waved her away and headed to the bathroom in the prison dorm. Inside, I encountered a row of toilets lined up next to one another without a barrier in between them or a door in front of them. I pictured the humiliation the women felt every time they had to relieve themselves. I forced myself to experience it. I sat on the toilet, trying to pee, the whole time feeling exposed and violated. I prayed no one would walk in on me.

I entered the shower room and imagined what it would be like to stand in this big open room crammed with other women.

In Alabama, male officers work in female prisons, and I'd already heard stories of them hooting and hollering at the prisoners, mocking the women's bodies.

"Oh, my," I whispered to myself, "I'd die in here because I'm fat and they'd make fun of my big behind."

I entered a stifling-hot room packed with cots. Since the dorm was nearly empty, I lay down on the bed. The mattress was one inch of nothing. The springs jabbed into my back and butt. And the thin blue wool blanket? I wondered how these women could sleep with that scratchy thing against their skin. It was so threadbare and worn. Did they ever get warm in the winter?

It could have been me in there.

After visiting regularly for a while, I became more accustomed to the prison life that was their world. Difficult as it was for an inmate to live there, it was prison after all, and their universal complaints—horrible food, loss of privacy, absence of freedom, endless monotony—started to fade. I came to accept what the place was.

But then I started to hear the women's stories. One by one they would share something with me about their past. One after another would confide in me. I *heard* their lives.

It hit me hard.

Some had been repeatedly raped and beaten since they were young. Many had been abused by angry boyfriends. Nearly every woman had suffered physical or sexual abuse from someone, many when they were just little girls. Many had children of their own when they themselves were still children.

It broke my heart.

At one time, I thought all people in prison deserved to be there. I thought they were all bad people who had done bad things. I had once believed that those people should get over their problems and simply choose to be productive.

Hearing their stories changed me. Yes, most of them had done bad things. But, oh my, most of them never had a fighting chance.

And who was I? I wasn't a "bad" person, even though I came within a whisper of being jailed myself. If you asked friends about me, they'd say I was a very good person. I'd donate clothes to the poor and write checks to charities. If I passed homeless people on the street, I'd give them money.

But the truth was, I'd also try to run away from them as fast as possible. Truth was, I didn't want to get too close. Truth was, I didn't want to look at them. Truth was, I blamed them for their predicaments. Truth was, I was devoid of sympathy for them. Truth was, I believed that these women had deserved what they were getting.

Now I knew their stories. What so many of them "got" was not anything anyone should ever get—as a child, as a young teenager, as a woman. They were survivors, and many were trying to live on, even though they barely had a chance.

After just a few weeks with the women, I became ashamed of the person I had been. When I heard their stories, I realized I had been judging them through my very limited, very personal perspective. I had seen them through my own past. For most of my childhood, I had been raised in a tiny trailer. I had made it, so why couldn't they? If I could overcome my adversities, why couldn't everyone?

Since these women couldn't turn their lives around, I had labeled them losers.

And then I learned how wonderful a chocolate-covered strawberry could be...

The fact that they had survived was a triumph. They were better than I was. I wouldn't have made it in their shoes. I would have curled up and died on the sidewalk.

I had come to the work release center to change women. Instead, they had changed me.

The more I got to know the women, the more I couldn't get them out of my head. I thought about them all the time. The work center—a place I'd barged into hoping they'd ask me to leave—was beginning to feel like a place I belonged. What began as volunteer work was starting to feel like something more.

Even though I was devoting time at the center, I was still working. We sold our tax business for a hefty sum, which we divided among the family. I started working with Jeff at his mortgage company and real estate business. I was still a hustler—we bought houses that were in foreclosure or bankruptcy, fixed them up, and sold them for profit—but my passion for making money was diminishing.

I'd pray with every woman who was about to be released. I was so happy for each one who was being given a second chance. They talked about building relationships with their children, many who had grown up without their mothers. They talked about making amends with family and friends they'd hurt along the way. They talked about finding jobs. They talked about finding a place to live. They talked about living life as a good Christian.

They were so excited that I'd get caught up in their enthusiasm. I believed maybe I had helped some of them turn their lives around and come closer to God. *Because of my help,* I thought, *these women will live right and do right. They will never be back.*

Only—then they'd come back.

"What are you doing back here?" I'd ask when I saw a woman I thought had left prison for good. "How did things get messed up so fast?"

"Oh, Miss Brenda. I didn't have anywhere to go. I didn't have anyone to help me," was the overwhelming response.

One after another would explain that when she was sent back to the place where she had committed her crimes, she wound up hanging out with the same friends she drank with or got high with or committed crimes with. Or she'd be back with the husband or boyfriend who beat her up.

"That can't be right," I said to one of the women. "Don't they have places for you to make some kind of transition?"

One woman told me about halfway houses: "It's a place to stay when you are half out of prison but not really anywhere else yet. But, Miss Brenda, most of the time people there get in more trouble than they do out on the street."

I thought about this. "Seems what you need is a 'whole-way' house. If I ever did this, I'd build me a whole-way house," I said.

She laughed. "I can see it now. Miss Brenda's gonna build herself a whole-way house."

I started doing research on the prison system. When a woman is released from prison, the Alabama Department of Corrections provides her with ten dollars, a really ugly prison-issued outfit—ill-fitting blue polo shirt and khaki pants—and a bus ticket back to her last known address, the place where she committed her crime.

According to the Bureau of Justice statistics, 30 percent of adult offenders released from state prisons are rearrested within the first six months of their release. Within three years of their release, this increases to 67 percent—that's two out of every three prisoners. I discovered that in Alabama 58 percent of the twenty-seven-thousand-plus inmates have served time before.

These people don't stand a chance.

I began to see that what these women so desperately needed was something that was not available to them. They needed a program that would help them change their lives, give them hope, and strengthen their faith. Halfway houses provide women with three hot meals and a shower but don't help them get back on their feet. They keep people in the problem. These women needed a place where they would receive help—spiritually, physically, emotionally, and educationally—a path *away* from the problem.

They needed a whole-way house.

I explained my vision to anyone who would listen. It seemed so simple to me. But everyone I spoke to—friends, family, the parole board—looked at me like I had gone crazy.

I had to be a little crazy to want to change the system.

Actually, I had to be a whole lot of crazy.

4

Blown Away

The most beautiful things in the world cannot be seen or even heard but must be felt with the heart.

HELEN KELLER

Jeff Spahn was a handsome California man with a big smile, a big personality, and an easygoing manner. I met him at a business conference in Birmingham. It was, well, *friendship* at first sight.

He was all business, and so was I. Divorced twice, I wasn't looking for love with a man six years my junior. Jeff, divorced for more than fifteen years, wasn't looking to fall in love again.

A few months later I ran into Jeff at another business conference. We had dinner. I found myself attracted to him. This very independent man was different from the good ol' Southern boys I was used to.

We dated long-distance for more than a year. We'd send each other those Hallmark cards showing little children dressed in adult clothing. That's how we made each other feel. We looked like adults, but inside we were children pretending to be adults. Jeff said that he could still see in me the redheaded girl with pigtails, freckles, and a gregarious personality.

At Christmas, Jeff came to Birmingham to spend the holiday with my family. As our time together was coming to an end, Jeff handed me an enormous box. I opened it. Inside was a smaller box. I opened that box. Again, there was another box. I kept tearing through boxes until I got to a very small square box. When I pulled open the lid, I saw the words, "Will you marry me?"

I didn't even look at the ring. I jumped up and screamed, *"Yes!"*

We were married on June 28, 1998, in front of our family and friends in a gazebo at Hob Hill, the beautiful house Jeff had bought for us a few months earlier.

Jeff was a real estate investor and a mortgage broker in California and Texas. When he decided to live in Birmingham with me, he sold his properties and re-invested his money in prime Gulf Shores beachfront real estate. One home Jeff purchased was called the Island Princess. With its wraparound porch that looked onto the bay, the house was a popular wedding venue and a top rental property in the area.

Like me, Jeff had grown up knowing one day he would be successful. He wanted to make his fortune and retire at thirty. But life had thrown him some curves. When he was twenty-five, he and his wife divorced. When we married, Jeff was forty-one and ready to get back to his goal of an early retirement. He and I agreed we'd work just a few more years and then settle permanently at our dream home in Gulf Shores. We balanced our work with a lot of play—we traveled to Europe, cruised the Caribbean, and spent as many long weekends as possible at the beach.

But two years into our marriage, I threw him my own curve. One of my clients told me that her drug-addicted daughter was pregnant with a boy and couldn't possibly raise the child. Did I know anyone who would want to adopt him?

Yes, I thought. *Me. I want to adopt him.*

Nine years earlier I'd had a dream about a baby boy I would adopt. It was so vivid that I had woken, convinced that this was more than a dream, that it was something that would really happen someday.

Years passed, and I forgot about it. But when my client asked me if I knew any people interested in adopting, I recalled this dream and realized this was what I wanted to do, what I felt I had to do. This was a baby who would have challenges—his mother was a drug addict, and he could be born with a barrage of health problems. I could help.

First I had to approach Jeff. I imagined he wouldn't be too thrilled initially, but I thought he might warm to the prospect. I'd break down my idea into little digestible pieces. With Jeff my motto was, "How do you eat an elephant? One bite at a time."

"One of my clients told me that her daughter is pregnant," I told him that day.

"Mmm-hmm."

"She asked me if I knew anyone who could adopt the child."

"Uh-huh."

"Wouldn't it be wonderful," I said, "if she could find someone she knew and trusted?"

"I guess."

I paused. "Jeff, what do you think of you and me adopting this baby?"

He laughed like this was a hysterical joke.

Then he saw my somber expression. I still remember how his eyes grew real wide and his face turned white. He was so shocked he couldn't speak. We had talked about retiring, not starting a family.

When he regained his composure, he shook his head. "Brenda, we're not adopting any baby. That's the craziest idea I've ever heard."

"I have to do this."

Jeff smiled as if something had dawned on him. "Brenda, what you have is empty nest syndrome. You're depressed because the kids are all growing up. You don't need a baby. You need a psychologist."

Now I was annoyed. "I do not have such a thing. I do not need to see a shrink."

"Yes you do."

Jeff and I made an agreement. We'd see a therapist and let the therapist determine whether or not I was crazy or suffering from any syndrome. We picked a random therapist from the phone book because Jeff was convinced I knew everyone in Birmingham and would somehow rig this in my favor. I met with the therapist by myself and then with Jeff.

"Your wife is not crazy," the therapist told Jeff after a few meetings. "She doesn't have empty nest syndrome. She simply feels strongly that this is something she is supposed to do."

I thought Jeff was going to lose it. He was so angry with the therapist, he could barely speak.

"You always win," he finally said to me.

A few months later, we watched as our tow-headed baby boy was born. He had trouble breathing and was whisked into intensive care.

Since Jeff had been so against this, we hadn't even picked out a name. But as we saw this precious newborn struggle for life, I could see Jeff's expression soften. He looked at our tiny infant with tubes sticking out of him. "My little Hunter's going to be just fine," he whispered, his eyes teary.

At that moment when he named his son, I knew he'd fallen in love with Hunter Thomas Spahn.

Retirement was delayed for Jeff yet again as we raised our newborn. But we would retire soon enough. And what better place for a little boy to grow up than on sandy Gulf Shores beaches?

A few years passed. We took some baby steps to prepare for our eventual move to the beach. We decided to downsize and purchased a smaller home in a new development in nearby Trussville. It was a smart move—as soon as we put our Hob Hill home on the market, we had a buyer willing to pay full price for it.

When I began ministering at the work release center, Jeff could feel our life plans undergoing a seismic shift. I stopped talking about retirement. I was focused on finding a solution to the high recidivism rate among female prisoners. Instead of working with Jeff in real estate, I was learning about reentry programs for recently released prisoners.

Each year, more than six hundred women are released from Alabama's prisons. Yet Alabama has no state-supported reentry housing or reentry employment programs. I found out there were a few community programs, but none were faith-based. I believed that without faith in God, a person had no hope. Without hope, there was no chance for a future.

Everyone I spoke to about my whole-way house idea—the parole board and treatment centers—seemed to think I was wasting my time. They all told me the same thing: "Just stick to prison visitation. Continue chatting with the women there. You're good at it and you'll be happier. This idea of yours is nothing but heartache."

As I did my research, I kept hearing about a man named Ken Garner. He was a program director at TASC—Treatment Alternatives to Street Crime—at the University of Alabama at Birmingham. Started in 1972, TASC was a national drug treatment program aimed at getting nonviolent offenders out of the criminal justice system and into treatment programs where they could receive the help they needed to escape the revolving door that prison becomes for so many. Ken was in charge of the just-developed Another Chance project, a grant-funded program through the Department of Justice. His job was to place female offenders in transitional settings after prison and before parole.

Many of the women at the work release center took classes at TASC and they all spoke highly of Ken. I kept hearing how Ken was the man who could make my idea happen.

I phoned him repeatedly, but he was always busy. I called and called and never heard back.

It seemed that door was closed.

Hurricane Ivan roared through the Gulf of Mexico, ripping up houses and flooding towns, while I was hosting back-to-back showings of *The Passion of the Christ* to the work release inmates. During intermission, I asked the women to pray that my beloved Island Princess would be spared. I wasn't too worried though—I trusted God.

I explained my beliefs to the women at the center: "If you have faith in God, He will protect you. I know my house will be fine."

The next day, Jeff, Matthew, Beau, and I drove out to the beach house to assess the damage. We couldn't reach it because of street flooding, so we drove across the bay to get a glimpse with our binoculars. Matthew, who at six foot five was the tallest among us, stood on a sand dune and surveyed the area. Our home was four houses from a bridge, so when Matthew found the bridge, he began to count the houses.

"Okay," he said, peering through the binoculars. "There's the bridge. There's the New Orleans couple's house. Okay, there's the house that belongs to the man from Virginia. There's your neighbor's from Colorado. And..."

He stopped. "Mom," he said hesitantly, "I don't know how to tell you this. Our house is gone."

"Give me those binoculars," I said. "The house is not gone!"

I squinted through the eyepiece and gasped. All that remained of our beautiful dream house was an enormous gap where it had once been. The neighbors' houses to the left and the right were perfectly intact. Our house was so obliterated that we didn't need a bulldozer to tear it down.

We learned later that in the midst of this hurricane, a tornado had vacuumed up our house and dumped it out at sea.

I dropped to my knees and started sobbing.

How did this happen? Those New Orleans people are complete heathens! They don't even believe in God. I prayed. I'm showing The Passion of the Christ, *for God's sake. This is the thanks I get?*

I was so angry at God for allowing this to happen. Well, I'd show God. *You take my house. Fine! I'll just build a new one!* I called an architect: "Draw me up a place that's even bigger and better than the last one."

A few weeks later as the architect was sketching plans, a man called. He offered to buy the lot for an obscene amount of money, especially considering that a few months earlier a buyer had called offering a lot less for the entire house. We accepted and paid off our mortgage. Amazingly, we had more left over than we ever could have imagined.

Still dizzy from our real estate windfall, we received a call from a real-estate agent that our Hob Hill home had fallen out of escrow. The buyer had just been diagnosed with throat cancer and needed to get out of the deal. And just like that, we were the owners—again—of our Hob Hill house.

I found myself alone one day at Hob Hill, which now was devoid of furniture. I began to feel ashamed of myself, my anger at God, my lack of faith in His provision. In such a short time, we had sold a house, bought a house, lost a house to a hurricane, and again owned the house we thought we had sold. We had been given so much, and yet I was so bullheaded in how I wanted everything to work out that I had failed to look for what God might have in mind.

But now, what would we do with this place? The Hob Hill house was so enormous. It was more like a hotel than a home. That's why we wanted to downsize in the first place. And then an idea suddenly dawned on me.

Hob Hill could be the location for my whole-way house plan.

I walked around, counting how many women could fit into bedrooms, the library, the dining room, and so many other rooms I had never figured out how to use very well when we had lived there. I became more and more excited. And it became clear what I needed to do.

The next day I marched straight into Ken Garner's office. I told his secretary that I wasn't budging until he came out to speak with me. The office staff looked at me like I was a very troubled woman—a woman who needed to be *in* a program, not *running* a program.

Finally a tall, handsome, well-dressed man came out and shook my hand. "I'm Ken," he said. "In your phone messages, you mentioned a plan."

I told him this was something I was called to do. I explained my idea for a whole-way house and the concept I had for really helping women coming out of prison. I explained that faith was a big part of it. I said this could be done differently and better.

After I was done, I waited to hear him laugh or tell me how crazy I was.

He paused, leaned back, and looked at me. He wasn't laughing. "Brenda," he said, "I think this is what I've been looking for." He explained that all the alternative programs focused on overcoming substance abuse. There was nothing faith-based. "These women have denounced their faith," he said. "They feel like they have no reason to believe. They are torn down. Someone like you, with your faith, could turn these women around."

We talked for a long while. He asked a lot of questions. I could see he was really intrigued. "This is very doable," he said finally.

The next day, Ken toured my house. He kept nodding his head as if he could visualize the program in action there. "You can house a lot of women here."

We stood, silent, in the vastness of the house.

"This could be amazing," he said.

Later, Ken had other members of TASC tour the house. He hired a UAB grant writer to put together a proposal for government funding, a perk I hadn't expected. Through this Another Chance grant, we were given thirty-five dollars per woman per day to cover some of their expenses. Ken became so involved that he helped paint the house, deliver furniture, set up the rooms, and drive the women right to my door that very first day.

But before I could begin any of this, I had to get Jeff to eat another elephant.

"Jeff," I said, "since the market is down a bit in Birmingham, maybe it's not really a good time to sell the Hob Hill house."

"Mmm-hmm."

"So, you know that idea I had for my whole-way house?"

"Uh-huh."

"I was thinking I could do it at the Hob Hill house."

"What?"

"The house is just sitting there, with no one making an offer."

"What?"

"And it's not like I'm going to run the program. I'll just check in on it every so often. I'll barely have anything to do with it."

"That's the craziest idea I've ever heard."

"Just let me try it. What's it going to hurt?"

"Brenda, you can't do this. I really don't know what you're thinking. It's not going to happen. Ever."

Poor Jeff. He thought he'd married the goose that laid the golden egg. But he wound up with a duck instead.

Jeff looked like he might just keel over and have a heart attack. After a long, long silence, he finally spoke, angrily. "Do it. But I'm not going to be there. I'm going to live in Gulf Shores until you get this crazy bug out of your system. You have no idea what you're doing. You're going to get yourself killed."

I watched my husband as he angrily stomped up the stairs. I knew I was asking too much from a man I'd already asked too much from. It wasn't fair of me to expect him to understand. I was putting my marriage at risk for a bunch of prisoners I didn't know. I wanted to run up after Jeff and tell him I was sorry, that I wouldn't go through with it.

But I didn't. I believed this was something I was meant to do. It might take some time, but Jeff would understand. He'd realize I knew what I was doing.

But *did* I know what I was doing?

5

The Girl Band

Like Alexander the Great and Caesar, I'm out to conquer the world. But first I have to stop at Walmart and pick up some supplies.

JAROD KINTZ

Melinda had taken the women upstairs to pick out bedrooms. I was downstairs, stinging from the defections of the staff I had carefully chosen and shocked by the selection of women the prison system had sent to me. This was a whole different level of convicts than I had dealt with at the work release center. I was truly fearful of them and concerned about my family in the same house with them.

Surprisingly, Melinda had been transformed since their arrival. Despite her own fears, she immediately took control, perhaps sensing that such women would never respect her authority unless she asserted herself. I could hear her talking with them, treating them like old friends who'd just arrived for a visit. She called them "sweetie." What had gotten into my little girl? She was so confident, so self-possessed, so believing in my plan.

I told myself I had to tell her she was very wrong to trust me—she could get herself killed.

Eventually Melinda led the women back downstairs, and soon they were sitting across from me in the library.

Melinda had to leave to take care of her young children at home. I had silently hoped she would be able to stay, but she smiled and said good-bye, and then was off. For a moment I thought I should tell her where my will was and where these women would most likely bury my body.

Just like that, I was alone with them. I really didn't know what to do. I had no plan beyond getting them here and then leaving them with the housemother.

The women stared at me, their arms folded, their expressions blank. I knew they were waiting for me to explain myself or tell them what I had planned or yell at them to get to work and do something—that's what they'd become accustomed to in prison.

I waited for someone to say something to me. I was hoping for perhaps a kind word, a thank-you, or some small expression of gratitude—something to put me at ease and soften the tension. No one spoke.

I knew that whatever I said next would be critical to any success I hoped to have with the women. Truly, it could make or break the program. I said a silent prayer, asking God to help me find the right words.

"Listen," I finally said. "I believe there are going to be thousands of women whose lives will be changed by what we are starting at this house today."

I looked around at the six of them. Some were staring at the ceiling, others at the floor. But no one interrupted me.

"If you don't want to be here, let me call whoever and get you out of this situation. But if you want to stay, let's make this work. God and society need this to work. God is calling us like we've never been called before. He wants believers like me to quit being afraid of getting their hands dirty and help women like you. And He wants you to see that there is hope. Because, trust me, there is hope. And what we do today and tomorrow and the next day could have a tremendous impact on the entire system. We could change the way it works. We could change women's lives. But I need you to help me. We have to join together or we will fail."

I put on a smile and nodded, but let me be honest: *I didn't believe anything I said.* In those moments, given the way this had started, I didn't believe this program would help thousands of women. I didn't think it could even help these six.

But the women started to nod. They seemed to like the idea that they were innovators.

I continued: "Your small bags of belongings, those are all the things that you have in the world. God wants you to have a whole lot more. He wants you to have wonderful things. And you will."

They seemed to really like this idea too. Some were nodding more vigorously.

All of these words just came out of me. I hadn't known what to say or how to say it. Knowing me, I had a real good chance of saying exactly the wrong things in the wrong way. But God gave me the words that were needed.

One image that afternoon had seared my heart. Each had arrived with just that one brown grocery bag. I hadn't expected them to show up with a truckload of Louis Vuitton suitcases, but I was shocked and heartbroken by how little they owned. It was next to nothing. Tomorrow, they wouldn't even have a pair of clean panties. I thought then of what I'd want to do if I were in their shoes.

"Let's go to Walmart!"

As we headed outside to the van, one of the women pointed to the word Loveladies, which I'd painted in pink across the side of the fifteen-passenger vehicle. "What are Loveladies?" she asked.

I explained. Lovelady was my maiden name. My daddy, James Kenneth Lovelady, had always been my biggest fan, my loudest supporter, the man who believed I could do anything I wanted to do. I was the apple of his eye, and I've always seen myself through those eyes. Because of my daddy, I believed I could do anything. When he died in 1995, I sat in my car after his burial and watched through tears as people went about their lives. I thought, *What a shame. The most wonderful man in the world just died, and these people don't even know it.* So I prayed to God that one day I would do something worthwhile. I vowed that whatever that was I would name it after my daddy. I wanted his name to live on after his death.

What better way to honor him than to name this program after him? The Lovelady Whole Way House. Could there be a better name for a women's program? If anyone believed this program would work, it would have been my daddy.

"You are a Lovelady," I said. "You all are the Loveladies."

I wasn't supposed to drive this enormous van. Truth is, over the years I had racked up too many speeding tickets. The car insurance would have doubled if my name were listed on it. But since my driver quit, I had no choice but to get behind the wheel.

"Faster, Mommy, faster!" Hunter screamed once we settled into our seats and started downhill. He loved when I'd play roller coaster with him and speed down our long, winding driveway.

The women were accustomed to the slow, overly cautious Department of Corrections drivers who make a point of driving way under the speed limit. As I pressed down on the accelerator and swerved into curves, tires screeching—in other words, driving normal—the women gasped. Hunter squealed with delight.

Only I'd never driven anything this big, and I was taking the bumps too fast. The van bounced into the air and then came back down, slamming into the road. The women screamed and held on to their seats. "Are you crazy, lady? You trying to get us all killed?"

I thought it wasn't a bad thing if for a change *they* were the ones scared for their lives.

When I had mentioned a trip to Walmart, the women became excited. They chattered about all the things they wanted to buy. For just a few moments, they weren't convicts but typical women about to go on a shopping excursion.

But they weren't typical women.

A chill ran through me. How could I keep up with six women in Walmart? What if I lost them? What if they ran away? What if they stole things? What if they scared the other customers? What if they threatened the other customers? Should I casually walk in to Walmart and ask the managers to lock all the doors because I had six women fresh out of prison with me? Should I get a security guard to chaperone us?

Again, I hadn't thought this through. Maybe going to Walmart was a big mistake.

"I'll give you each one hundred dollars," I said as I steered the van into the Walmart parking lot. "Buy things you need: panties, soap, cosmetics, and any groceries you want."

"I thought you said we were going to Walmart. They don't sell food there."

"Walmart sells everything."

"You're lying," they said incredulously.

"I'm not lying. There's a grocery store on one side and a pharmacy next to it. Then there's all that other stuff—clothes, toys, furniture." I paused. "Haven't y'all ever been to a Walmart before?"

"Hey, lady," Shay spit out. "Don't you talk to us like we're stupid. 'Course we've been to a Walmart before."

"Hush. I don't think you're stupid."

Then it dawned on me. This was 2004, and Shay had been in prison for most of the last twenty years. In 1984, there were no megastores or cell phones or e-mail. Most people hadn't heard of CD players. Most people didn't know what an Apple Mac was. And back then, Walmart didn't sell groceries. These women were Rip Van Winkles looking at the world for the first time in a long, long while.

I had learned in the work release center that unlike their male counterparts, female inmates don't get many visitors to keep them updated on the world. I found out later that most of my women had had no visitors. For them, walking in to a 150,000-square-foot superstore that sold everything you could possibly imagine was like landing on another planet.

"Excuse me, are you a band?" a young woman in the parking lot called to us as we were climbing out of the van. I was confused—did this group of hardened criminals in their oversized prison-issued blue polo shirts and baggy khaki pants in any way resemble a rock band? Then I looked at the side of the van with Loveladies written in script on the side.

This woman thought we were an all-girl group, a bunch of rocker chicks in between concert dates.

A bit of my nervousness evaporated. For a few fleeting seconds I forgot they were just released from prison. We were The Loveladies, an all-girl rock band.

Ready to wreak havoc on Walmart.

"Something like that, darlin'," I said.

As soon as the glass doors slid open, I decided the best way to handle it would be to just get out of their way. In their excitement, they'd probably run me over with their carts. What happened after, we'd just have to figure out.

But when I turned around, the six stood frozen at the front of the store, their mouths hanging open in disbelief.

"What you lookin' at?" Shay snapped at some woman strolling by us. The woman looked away and picked up her pace.

"Shay, she wasn't looking at you. You're going to get us kicked out of here," I said.

"Well, she shouldn't be staring at us."

"She wasn't."

"Yes she was," Shay said. "She knows...everyone knows."

"What does everyone know?"

"They're all staring at us because they know we just got outta jail."

I laughed. "They know nothing. If anything, they think we're part of a rock band. Look, I'm getting a cart. Hunter and I are gonna look at the toys. You go get your stuff and meet me back here in thirty minutes."

I grabbed a cart, picked up Hunter, and strapped him in front. When I looked back to wave at the women, they were still standing in the same spot, staring at me.

"All right, y'all go on now. The underwear's that way." I pointed at the lingerie section as I pushed toward the toy aisle.

I turned around again. They still hadn't moved.

Other shoppers were gaping, probably trying to make sense of why I was shooing six paralyzed black women over to the panty aisle.

Shay walked toward me.

"Yes?"

"I'm coming with you."

"Why?"

"I wanna see the toys."

"Why the heck would you want to look at toys?"

"What's wrong with that? I like toys."

"What? I don't get it. You've all been locked up for years and years. You have your freedom and you have a hundred dollars to spend. And you want to look at toys? Give me a flippin' break."

Even as I spoke, I detected in Shay's expression something I hadn't noticed before. All that fierceness, that anger, that hate was really just a mask to hide her fear. Shay Curry was terrified. All these women were terrified. They had been incarcerated for so long that they'd lost their dignity and their self-respect, if they had ever had any in the first place.

They believed that "normal" folks around them could smell the stench of Tutwiler on them. They believed that others saw them the way they saw themselves—as losers, rejects, and outcasts who belonged behind bars and would most likely be back behind them soon.

They were AIS—Alabama Institutional Serial—numbers. After all, that had been their names for decades. It had been etched on to all their prison clothing. It had been seared into their souls. The prison had stripped them of everything, even their humanity.

"You're afraid," I said as I stared at Shay.

Shay angrily narrowed her eyes. "Lady, don't you say that to us. We're not afraid." But this time she wasn't yelling. Her voice was almost a whisper.

I smiled at her and lowered my voice. "That's bullcrap, Shay. You're even more scared of me than I am of you."

She shook her head. "You're one crazy white lady."

We stood in silence: a crazy white lady, six terrified black ladies, and a little boy. "You know what?" I said. "We're probably all a little scared. So let's shop together."

The women looked relieved. Even Shay's scowl softened.

Each held on, grabbing my cart or my bag or a piece of my clothing. I was taken aback when one of the women held my hand. They walked so close to me—all of them—I could barely move.

Slowly we shuffled all together to the Walmart panty section.

"We can get anything we want? What's the catch?"

"There is no catch," I said.

Each woman grabbed some white panties out of the bins and headed back to the cart.

"Actually there is a catch," I corrected myself. "No white panties."

"What? Why?"

"Because that's all you could wear in prison. You're out of prison, so it's time to dress different, even down to your underwear."

"Could you pick them out for us?" one asked.

"Yeah, Miss Brenda, pick us some panties."

I shook my head in disbelief. In prison, every single decision was made by someone else on their behalf. They had completely lost the ability to make even the simplest of decisions. Even though I knew it would be easier and faster if I just grabbed them all some underwear or let them buy plain white ones, I also knew they had to start making decisions if they were to survive outside prison. So why not start with panties?

"No. I'll help you, but you have to pick them."

Soon there was pandemonium in the panty section. The women pulled underwear out of the bins. I hadn't thought until that moment how many choices the women faced when choosing underwear: Hiphuggers. Boxers. Briefs. High cut. Low cut. Bikini. Thong. Pastels. Bright colors. Solids. Stripes. Polka dots. Florals. Plaids. Geometrics. Lace. Plain.

"What the heck are these?" One of the women held up a pair of thongs. "Why would you wear something that goes up your butt?"

The women were giggling. "How long have they been wearing these in the free world?"

"The free world's gone crazy."

"How can that even be comfortable?"

I'd never heard the term "free world" before. Since some hadn't been in the free world for decades, they didn't even know how to figure out their panty size. I had to show each one how to read the tags inside and decode sizes for them. They held them against their waists and laughed. "I couldn't get my butt in this," someone said.

They were all talking so loud we quickly had an audience. Regular shoppers couldn't figure why a group of grown women were so fascinated by panties.

"Come on. Y'all are going to get us kicked outta here."

"Can't we just get some white drawers? This is too hard."

"It's not hard. Just pick something," I said. "You're not going to marry it."

They laughed like this was the funniest thing they'd ever heard. I felt they were beginning to see me as more than just a crazy, red-haired white lady. Now they were seeing me as a *funny,* crazy, red-haired white lady.

It took more than an hour to pick out panties and bras. The women didn't want their own carts, so they each made separate piles for their underwear in my cart. "Keep your stuff on your side," they'd snap at each other. "Hey, your panties are touching my panties."

Hunter and I couldn't stop laughing. Hunter thought this was all a big game. He'd toss one person's underwear into someone else's pile. He'd nearly burst with laughter as he waited for the women to react.

"He's messed up our piles," they whined to me. "Hunter, you leave our things alone now."

I'd rearrange the piles in the cart until the women simmered down. Then Hunter would laugh and reach for the panties.

"You stop it, Hunter," I said, but he knew I didn't really mean it, and we both giggled.

Next we shopped for toiletries. In prison, the women washed their hair and bodies with state soap—a stick of lye soap that left them feeling dirtier than when they began washing. Naturally, it was the same thing all over again, each one grabbing a bar of plain white soap. I told them to put the plain soap back and find body wash instead. Most had never heard of body wash and didn't understand how a liquid could really clean you. They insisted on a bar of plain soap, but I refused: "You're living in the free world now. You have lots of choices."

I showed them rows and rows of body wash. They stared in complete confusion—again, we don't realize how many choices we sort through when we shop.

They opened some bottles and sniffed the contents, commenting on each scent: "That's nasty."

"This is a good one."

"Who would want to smell like this?"

"This is mine, not yours." If someone loved a smell, she'd declare it hers—meaning no one else was allowed to get it. They'd pass around the bottles and argue over which body washes smelled the best—lavender or vanilla, grapefruit or coconut. I would run to the bottles they'd abandoned on the shelves and screw on the caps they'd removed, certain that any minute security would escort us out.

At some point, I stood back and watched. I felt like a kid at the movies—all I needed was a big bag of popcorn. They were toddlers, delighting in the smell of lilacs and lavender and lemons and vanilla. They hadn't smelled fragrances like this in years, if ever. A gathering crowd watched them again, trying to make sense of this scene—a motley crew of women savoring the smells of cheap body wash.

Now the women didn't seem to notice the stares. They were reveling in the joys of the free world.

I found myself in awe of this. How we take our freedom for granted. Something as mundane as the scent of body wash can be a simple joy. We barely notice the wonderful smells we breathe in every day; we aren't thankful for them. But to women who had been locked up for decades and decades, the simple act of sniffing fragrances was a powerful symbol of freedom. It occurred to me how their world had been filled with the horrible stench of incarceration—lye soap, body odor, prison food, institutional cleaners. Breathing in lilac and lavender and coconut and citrus was like taking a big whiff of freedom.

"I don't want nobody taking my hygienes," one of the women yelled.

"Hygienes?" I asked.

"Hygienes," one of them said, as if that explained everything.

They were so worried that one of the other women would claim their hygienes that we visited the office supply section for a few pens. The women wrote their initials on their panties, body washes, and lotions.

"Are you sure it's okay?" one of them asked. "You're spending all your money on us."

This was Tiffany—the one who had held my hand. She'd been repeating this question to me each time she hesitantly added an item to the cart. "Is this okay? You shouldn't be spending all this money on me, on any of us. Why are you doing this?"

I could tell Tiffany was different from the rest. While the others entered my house brimming with anger, Tiffany had smiled and seemed euphoric with joy. She was tall and heavy but moved like a small person; she was here, there, and everywhere.

Tiffany had told me as I wheeled the cart through the store that she had never dreamed of a life without prison.

By the time we reached the checkout, we had been shopping for more than three hours. My feet were killing me; I was exhausted. Each woman had her products rung up separately. They wanted to make sure they got as close to one hundred dollars as possible. If someone's total came in a little less, they'd look around the checkout racks to see what they could add to their purchases—a candy bar, a pack of gum, anything—so they hit one hundred dollars.

"One hundred and six dollars," the cashier announced to one of the women. I told her she'd have to put back some things. She started crying. The poor cashier looked at me, confused. I shrugged my shoulders. "Okay, just leave it."

"That's not fair," the rest barked. "Now we get six more dollars."

"We're going to go back and get more stuff."

"No. We are done. I am not shopping for another minute," I said. "You can argue about this all the way home, but I am done."

"Miss Brenda, if you need me to put back some things," Tiffany said, "I will."

"No, Tiffany, you can keep all your things. Let's just get going home."

Home. My house was now these women's home.

As we left, Tiffany turned toward me.

"Miss Brenda, I think lots of people were staring at us."

I smiled. From the moment we had walked in to the store until we climbed back into the van, we had had an audience struggling to decipher who we were and what we were doing.

"Yes, Tiffany, lots of people *were* staring at us. But they were just jealous. They don't have what we have."

Unlike my earlier speech at the house, this time I meant every word of it. I knew we had a lot of work ahead of us and there were a lot of struggles to overcome, but I also knew I was finally doing what God had told me to do.

I had walked into Walmart feeling afraid and uncertain, believing I'd made the biggest mistake of my life. I walked out of Walmart feeling brave and confident, believing I was walking into the destiny God had for me.

I smiled harder than I had in a long, long time.

6

Shay

There are very few monsters who
warrant the fear we have of them.

ANDRE GIDE

I know it sounds nuts that a grown woman couldn't pick out drawers, but I couldn't. I'd see a pair I liked. Then I'd see another that I liked better. It just seemed that no matter what ones I picked, there would always be something better. There were so many designs and colors.

The store was so big and filled with so many people. I was used to being squeezed in a dorm room with hundreds of women. But they were my kind and I got used to it. These people at the store were all better than me. They stared at us, and I could tell they knew our story. I felt like I had my AIS number—118074—stamped on my forehead.

I just wanted to get some white underwear—that's all I'd worn in prison—but Miss Goody Two-Shoes wouldn't let me. So I got me a pack of Hanes briefs in different colors.

On the van ride home, I didn't feel like listening to those other women babbling on and on about how great this all was, so I thought about what color drawers I'd wear the next day. I couldn't even figure that out.

I thought about the drive from Tutwiler to Crazy Lady's house. These idiots had all been bursting with excitement. They believed all the lies Mr.

Garner was telling us. He said this do-gooding woman was going to help us get our lives together in her big house.

How did I get stuck with so many dimwitted women?

"Shut up. You're all making fools of yourselves," I yelled. The women were giggling like I used to when I was a little girl and believed handsome Uncle Benny's lies. They looked at me all hurt. Better to be hurt by the truth now than be disappointed by all the lies that some white lady was telling the parole board. They might believe her crap, but I was way too smart for her.

After two hours in a car with those idiots, we got to Birmingham. Mr. Garner turned on to a narrow, curvy street and then up a long driveway. He stopped halfway up the drive to make sure we took it all in.

"This is your new home," he said. I looked up to the left. Sitting on the hill was the most beautiful house I could imagine—buttery yellow, like frosting on a cake. It looked like Mrs. Carrington's house in *Dynasty.* Of course these stupid women oohed and aahed.

"Mr. Garner, you fooled us. You're taking us to work as slaves on a plantation," I said.

"No. That's your new home."

The women all giggled, which made my anger boil over. I hated these stupid women almost as much as the white lady we were about to become servants for.

"Keep it up. Y'all fixin' to be maids up there, living in a shack out back."

That did the trick. Soon they all had that defiant look, that attitude I wanted to see. I was proud of how they listened to me and considered me the leader. The six of us were old-timers and had been together for years. I was grateful for that because people less seasoned might fall for this scam.

"That's the Lovelady Whole Way House," Mr. Garner said as he drove toward it.

"Lovelady ho'way house is more like it," I said. I couldn't stop laughing at my joke, but the other women just stared ahead, their mouths like straight lines.

As we topped the driveway, I saw a woman with a mane of curly red hair peeking out a window. I guess she wanted to get a good glimpse at her slaves. I looked around the property. In the back where I thought there would be shacks was a swimming pool surrounded by beautiful grounds with flowers and trees, patios, and plenty of lawn furniture. The idiots with me began giggling again.

"This is the most beautiful house I've ever seen," they said at once.

My anger boiled up again, so bad I felt like I would explode. "Don't you know it's not going to work that way for us? No way are they taking us out of prison and putting us in a place like this. We're being tricked. Get ready for your little black dress and white apron."

"Well then, hand me a broom! I don't care if I'm a maid," Tiffany said. "This is a miracle from God, and I'm gonna take it."

I'd known Tiffany from prison. So naive. But she was my baby. A big baby. She reminded me so much of Carolyn, my best friend growing up who went through all that bad stuff with me. I had bonded with Tiffany right away in prison. But I also knew her real well: I knew she wanted drugs more than this house.

That redheaded lady stared at us, and I made sure to look as tough as possible when I got out of the van. I wanted her to know I was in charge. I wanted her to get a really good look at the scowl on my face. I did that thing I learned to do with my eyes and my mouth. I could practically turn my face into a fist. It always worked. People would get out of my way and leave me alone when I pulled that look out of my bag of tricks.

These simple-minded women were all tripping over each other to get inside.

"Welcome to my home," redhead woman exclaimed. "It's now your home also."

You've gotta be kidding me. Is this nut for real? Who in their right mind would bring a bunch of convicts to her home? With a little kid too? What kind of whacko is she? What kind of game is she playing with the system?

She told us her name was Brenda, and the other women immediately called her Miss Brenda. It made me really mad that my bad face that scared everyone didn't seem to bother her. She was so dumb. Did she not know that we were a bunch of hardasses who could hurt her and her kid?

I went upstairs with her daughter, Melinda, who had the bluest eyes and the kindest face I'd ever seen in my life. Something about her eyes got to me, so I avoided looking at them. She was so soft-spoken as she showed us the bedrooms. How could she treat us this way? Like we were just normal people staying at her home? "Sweetie"? Who calls convicts "sweetie"? Her voice dripped with what sounded like love. But she was probably as nuts as that red-haired mother of hers.

At the top of the steps was a yellow room filled with sunlight. It was the most beautiful bedroom I'd ever seen. The word Peace was painted on a plaque on the door. The bed looked so comfortable I had to sit on it. Oh, my Lord in heaven, it felt so good. I couldn't even remember the last time I had a bed with a real mattress. Who am I kidding? I never had a real mattress before. I pulled the cover back and saw that it was Posturepedic. I didn't want to move because I was afraid it would go away. I knew there were still other rooms to see, but what if this was the best and someone took it away from me?

"This is my bed," I said in my mean voice so those dimwits would be too afraid to touch it. I had claimed my territory, and I was not budging until everyone had their beds. No one was taking this away from me. I felt like a child—I was so excited about that mattress. But I made sure not to show it.

Later, Miss Goody Two-Shoes rambled on to us about how good God was. I wanted to scream at her right then and there. The anger began boiling again. I wasn't having anything to do with God because He could have helped that little girl years ago.

This time I decided to keep my mouth shut. I did not want to lose that bed.

7

The Other Visitor

Darkness cannot drive out darkness;
only light can do that.
Hate cannot drive out hate;
only love can do that.

MARTIN LUTHER KING JR.

I stood at the stove cooking french toast for *seven* women—another, Quincey, had arrived a few hours after the others. Cooking gave me time to pull my thoughts together.

I adored Tiffany. She was a big teddy bear who greeted everyone with a smile. She called us all Suga and was so accommodating, so ready to sooth flaring tempers or referee arguments. I knew she wanted this plan to work as much as I did. She was worried the women would mess up and I'd send them back to prison, so she overcompensated with cheeriness. She was like a tall sunflower in a garden of weeds.

From the way she expressed herself, I had gotten an impression she'd had a charmed life that had taken bad detours. I reviewed her history and was surprised to learn she had almost no education. Many programs had attempted to rehabilitate her, but everyone had given up. The file deemed her a hopeless case. It stated she had no future without institutionalization. But this file didn't reflect the woman in front of me who was always singing or humming. Tiffany was filled with such joy. I couldn't imagine what had gone wrong. How could she have wound up in prison? What had happened?

I discovered that Tiffany couldn't do much of anything. She couldn't make a bed. She couldn't clean her clothes. That morning, I asked her to boil water and she gave me a blank expression.

"Boil water." She sounded perplexed, as if I'd asked her to perform surgery.

"You put water in a pot and turn on the stove," I explained, trying to stifle my shock.

How can you not know how to boil water?

"I'll do it for you, Mama," Charmain said, grabbing a pot.

Charmain—a rough confection of arrogance and neediness. She had strutted into the house and surveyed each room as if determining whether it would meet her criteria. She was the brat of the bunch, a spoiled twenty-something who had made a lot of money as a big-time drug dealer. At one time, she'd had fancy cars and expensive clothes. She was smart enough never to use the dope she sold but not smart enough to avoid getting caught. She had just served three years at Tutwiler for distribution of narcotics.

Despite this worldliness, she was like a little girl. That first night, Charmain had asked me to tuck her into bed.

"So now that I'm living in your house, are you my mama?" she asked.

I thought she was joking, but she stared at me seriously, her eyes big and hopeful. How could this convicted drug dealer seem so innocent, vulnerable?

Thinking she didn't really mean it quite so literally, I had replied, "Sure. You can consider me like your mama."

That first morning, she just wanted to please me. She boiled the water. She took out the pots and pans. As soon as I was finished with a utensil or a bowl, she'd swoop in and clean it. She'd even clean a clean glass before she'd use it.

"You don't have to do that," I said.

"It's okay. That's what daughters do for their mamas," she said.

Some of the other women caught on and started calling me Mama too.

Quincey shook her head and sighed as if these women were the biggest bunch of idiots. "She ain't your mama." Quincey didn't think she belonged here. "You can do nothing for me," she had said. "I don't need anything from you."

Quincey was small. Even her voice was tiny. But what she lacked in stature, she compensated for in attitude. She came from a more privileged background—she had a mother and father, which was enough to set her apart from the others—and maybe that made her feel she was better than the others. No matter what any of the girls said or did, she'd snap at them, like they were just the dumbest people she'd ever met. I thought of her as a snapping turtle, one who just might bite off my head if I got her angry enough.

"She's my mama," Charmain repeated.

"She's just some crazy lady," Quincey said. "She ain't my mama. I already got a mama. I don't need another one. I just wanna get out of here and get my life back. I'm tired of all these people telling me what to do."

"I got a mom. I definitely don't want this one too," said Suzanne, whose mother had already stopped by to drop off suitcases of clothes and a cell phone for her. "I shouldn't even be here."

Suzanne, who was a passenger in a car during a fatal drive-by shooting, didn't believe she should have been sent to prison, much less my home. She didn't think she was guilty of anything, except being in the wrong place at the wrong time.

I whisked my batter and pretended not to hear their whispers around the table.

"Why are we here anyway?" Quincey said.

"It don't matter. We've gone from pen to penthouse," said Melissa, who was thirty-five, tall, and stunningly beautiful. Melissa's addiction to cocaine had gotten her into trouble with the law. She'd been in and out of Tutwiler for possession and theft. "Pen to penthouse," she repeated.

Within the whispered chatter I heard, "That b**** is scammin' the system."

What? I wanted to scream. I continued cooking. I'd know that voice anywhere.

Parthina. Parthina didn't talk much, so she was hard to read. When she did talk, she spoke in a very squeaky voice. To me, the sound was like nails on a chalkboard—so irritating. Parthina was suspicious of me and Melinda. Any chance she'd get, she'd explain to the women that I was making a fortune off of them. But when she was around me, she didn't speak at all. She had been on crack forever, deemed a hopeless case by the parole board.

"She's fixin to get rich off us," Quincey whispered.

"I don't care what she's doin'. I wanna stay. It's like I died and went to heaven," Tiffany said.

I heard someone let out a mean laugh.

"She ain't just scammin' the system. That b**** is scammin' us too. You wait and see. This is some kind of trick and you're all acting like fools."

Shay spoke and the whispering stopped. It was hard for me to keep my mouth shut, but I continued dipping the bread into the batter as if I hadn't heard a word. I already knew how often these women had received false promises. Nothing I could say could convince them that I wanted to help them. They'd just have to see for themselves. But out of all of the women, Shay was testing me the most.

I'd already pegged Shay as a happiness vacuum. She would walk into a room and suck any joy out of it. Even Tiffany would stop singing around her. Shay had had no visitors and no money in prison—except for the twenty-five cents an hour she made sewing prison uniforms in the prison factory—so she had learned to con even the toughest convicts out of their possessions. She kept the other women terrified of her. She'd take their things, and no one would say a word. She'd already swiped poor Tiffany's Vaseline. Tiffany just smiled like it never happened.

Shay had been in prison for so long she herself had become a prison—with a big wall around her covered in sharp barbed wire. If you got too close, you'd probably wind up bleeding to death.

Shay. Suzanne. Tiffany. Quincey. Melissa. Charmain. Parthina.

Those were my magnificent seven.

I learned quickly that another visitor had stepped off the van with them when they arrived at my door. She was a dark, looming presence that had incredible control over all of them. She became an insidious virus that would never completely leave their system.

Tutwiler.

Built in 1942, Julia Tutwiler Prison for Women was named in honor of the "angel of the stockades." Tutwiler, a noted Alabama educator, crusaded for inmate education and improvement of prison conditions. But the prison has not lived up to its namesake's legacy.

In 2003, a year before the women were released to me, a judge ruled that because of its severe overcrowded conditions—there were 1,300 inmates in a prison designed to house 950—Tutwiler violated the US Constitution. In 2007, Tutwiler was named the most dangerous women's prison in the country by the Department of Justice, which also found that Tutwiler incurred the highest rate of sexual assault among women's prisons. The corrections officers—most of them men—regularly abused, sexually harassed, and even raped female inmates with few, if any, consequences.

The women live in fear every day they are confined there.

If you're a prisoner fresh off the bus, you enter Tutwiler from the back, through what the women refer to as a chicken coop because it's covered in barbed wire. As you stand there waiting to go through processing, inmates scream, "Fresh meat! Fresh meat!"

From there, you head to a processing room where you are roughly stripped, searched, forced to squat, cough, and bend over. Then your body and every orifice is sprayed with lice shampoo. If your hair is touching your shoulder, the guard yanks it into a ponytail with his hands and hacks it off with a pair of rusty scissors. Before you can recover from the shock of this, you are given your AIS number and your wardrobe—a white long-sleeve blouse, a white jacket, and white pants with your AIS number stamped on each like a logo. Written on the back of your clothes are the words "Alabama Department of Corrections."

You are officially a J3—prison lingo for inmate.

When you enter the prison, all you feel is the noise. The place is so loud it echoes inside you, as if a prison sound system is wired to your brain. The big metal door opens, you go through, and the door clangs shut behind you as a buzzer sounds. The clanging and buzzing bounce off the dingy gray linoleum floors and the paint-peeled cinder block walls. A second door opens and clangs. Everything echoes, everything reverberates—even a whisper, although the officers never whisper. When they bark at you—and that is all they do—it sounds like they are screaming through a megaphone. Their voices do not sound human.

As you walk down the loud, echoing hallway, you're told not to make eye contact with the guards, the officers, the wardens. You're also told not to walk in the middle of the hallway, where the big red line is. That area is reserved for members of the free world. So you slink along the walls, trying to be invisible, staring at the floor.

You're assigned to one of nine dorms, each designed to house 115 to 150 women, but because of overcrowding, your dorm may be crammed with 180. On both sides are bathrooms with toilets next to each other and no partitions. There's a big open shower room. You're allowed one small drawer for all your personal items. You're assigned a small bunk bed.

Breakfast is at 4:00 a.m., but you will learn fast that no one really goes to breakfast. Lunch is at 10:30 and dinner is at 3:30. You pick up a plastic tray and line up for chow in the commissary. There are always about sixty people in line.

As you wait, staff members yell at you to hurry up. When you get your food, the staff is still yelling. By the time you sit down at a wobbly metal table and chair, you have fewer than five minutes to eat. There are not enough seats for everyone. You eat sloppy joes—which most inmates call sloppy hoes—or slickmeat, which is some undistinguishable meat of unknown origin that is circular, slimy, and ranges in color from purple to burgundy. You really have no idea what you're eating.

When the last person in line gets her food, you're cramming as much into your mouth as you can on the way to the trash, where you empty your tray of uneaten food and head out. Most likely you are still hungry.

At 3:30 in the afternoon, dinner is so early that you're hungry for another meal before lights out. If you are lucky, you might be able to pay for Spam or ramen noodles or cheese curls at the prison store; if you have family, you might have a care pack from family by your bed. If you're willing to sell your soul, you might figure out ways to make money for food, soda, or even a pack of cigarettes.

Lights out is at 10:30, a misnomer because the lights are never really out. You sleep in a narrow cot with a peeled metal frame and a mattress so thin the springs stab at you. Your blanket is threadbare and worn and scratchy; it doesn't keep you warm. Your cot is so narrow you can't move. Your body hangs over the side. In order to block out the lights and the noise, you probably rely on some type of drug prescribed to alleviate anxiety and help you sleep. Most everyone at Tutwiler is on some kind of prescription drug, even prisoners arrested for narcotics use. Likely you'll spend your prison sentence in a drug-induced state. This fits the place—at Tutwiler, you are not quite dead but not really alive either.

And if you do manage to fall asleep, you never know if you'll have to "fireman" it—go from sleep to wide awake in a matter of seconds. You could be jolted awake in the middle of the night for a shakedown. Thirty correctional officers (C/Os) will turn on all the lights while screaming at you to get up. They say it's to search for contraband, but it's really so the C/Os can terrorize you. You're in an altered state—your mind is groggy with sleep—but your heart pounds fast with fear. You're herded into a big room where you have to get naked, squat, and cough in front of your dorm mates and the male C/Os.

When you get back into your dorm, your beds have been taken apart, your drawers have been ripped out, and your meager belongings have been thrown everywhere. Before you can go back to sleep, you're ordered to put your things back. By the time you reassemble your space, it's time to begin the day.

It's like the guards enjoy watching you suffer. The hate bubbles inside you. You try to push it down.

In winter, the prison is cold. But the worst times is summer, when it's so hot and humid even the cinder block walls drip with sweat. In Wetumpka, temperatures soar into the nineties; and in August, temperatures can hit three digits, but there is no air conditioning for the inmates. You might be able to sneak into the showers fully clothed midday for a little relief.

Once, on a ninety-two-degree day, I visited Tutwiler. As I walked in, I felt I'd entered a sauna. Everyone and everything was sweating. It was the most miserable feeling I have ever had. (Awhile after I had started my program, a woman was sent to me with a huge scar across her neck. When I asked her about it, she told me a woman had cut her throat because she would not share her fan. I thought about how hot I had been that terrible day in August and felt that if I'd been in her situation, I might have gotten my throat slashed too.)

The mostly male C/Os treat you like you're a dog. They call you by your number so often that you forget you have a name. They're everywhere and you have no privacy. There are no doors or barricades in the showers or toilets (many of which don't work). The C/Os are supposed to adhere to a knock-and-announce policy, but they don't. They walk right in on you as you sit on the toilet. People talk about losing freedom in prison, but losing privacy is just as bad—at times worse. The officers leer at you while you shower. They make nasty comments about your body. They joke about your breasts, your butt, your fat. You feel bad about yourself as it is, but they remind you that you can always feel worse.

"It smells like a can of sardines in here," they yell at you in the showers.

To get rid of your stench, you scrub your body as hard as possible with your bar of state soap—but you never feel clean. The bar leaves you feeling gritty, greasy, and even dirtier than when you started washing.

You see things you never could have imagined. You see male guards beat women. You see them drag women down the hallways by their hair. You see them rape other prisoners, but you can't say a word—they may rape you. You see women doing things to other women with their bodies, with their hands, with tubes of toothpaste wrapped tautly in ace bandages.

It will haunt you for the rest of your life.

Then one day, you're released.

You breathe in the clean, fresh air of rural Alabama. You are free, but you soon realize that Tutwiler holds on to you with its barbed-wire tendrils no matter where you go.

Even if you're staying at a home filled with sunlight, warmth, and love.

Even if the woman who greets you doesn't scream at you but speaks about a new life, about God, about starting over.

Even if this woman truly believes that with hope and love and God, people can change.

I was so naive. At first I didn't see those invisible hands that pulled at the women. But the remnants of Tutwiler were everywhere: in the way they walked with their eyes cast downward, their bodies nearly skimming the walls; the way they kept the bathroom door open as they sat on the toilet or took a shower; the way they kept turning the lights on during the night; the way they ate my famous french toast—as if any second I would take their food away.

"My Lord, y'all eat too fast," I said as they gobbled up their french toast as quickly as I set it down for them. They fought to get their plates first. They were afraid I wouldn't make enough for all of them. They were afraid they wouldn't get seconds. Or thirds.

"Slow down."

They looked at me like they had no idea what I meant.

"This is how we always eat," Tiffany explained. "We only got five minutes for meals."

"You're not in prison anymore. You can all slow down."

They eyed me for a second. Then they pushed their plates as close to the edge of the table as possible, lowered their heads, practically hugged the dish with one arm, and then scooped up the food so fast their forks were a dizzying blur. Then they were done, standing up and wondering what was next. In prison, there was always something next.

Suzanne was the only one still eating. She ate slow and proper, as if unaffected by those eight years at Tutwiler, as if those eight years had never happened.

"You're not going anywhere. First of all, you cannot leave until everyone is finished," I said. "You're going to slow down and learn to have conversations like a family. You're out of prison. You can take as long as you want to eat. From now on, we're going to sit at these tables for a half hour, no matter if we're done or not. And you don't need to get up so early either. There's no reason to be up at flippin' four in the morning."

"That's the time we always get up."

"How can you even sleep with all those lights on?"

When we went to bed the night before, I had turned off all the lights. By the time I'd gone to bed (where the housemother was supposed to sleep), almost every single light in the house was blazing. I got up and turned them off, but when I woke up that morning, they were all on again.

"I need lights on to fall asleep."

"I'm scared of the dark," Charmain said, nearly crying.

And how did *I* sleep in that house with seven ex-cons? If you had asked me that question when the women had arrived, I would have said I wouldn't dare close one eye around those horrible women, especially Shay. But at Walmart, something happened: I got a glimpse into their hearts. I knew they weren't the scary convicts who stomped into my home. I looked at Shay and no longer saw Shaved Head; I peered into those eyes and saw a woman who had been injured by life. Her words were still mean and cruel, but instead of listening to them, I heard the cry of her heart.

I thought God had abandoned me when the housemother quit. But when I looked into Shay's eyes, I felt as if I'd been catapulted into her soul, and I realized that God hadn't been absent or silent at all. Instead, He'd blessed me with an incredible gift—a clear view into their hearts. He wanted me here.

Before bed, I even hugged Shay. And while she did not hug me back—actually her body was as rigid as a board—she let out a long sigh, like a tire releasing its air. She needed to be hugged more than anything, but she didn't want me to know.

I asked each of them a question that night: "How long since you have been happy?"

Some said never. Some said they couldn't remember. Then Tiffany, sweet Tiffany, chimed in. "Walmart."

"Walmart," the others echoed excitedly. Their faces brightened as they recounted our expedition. This little journey had given them much more than toiletries and underwear. It had given them hope. No one can be truly happy until they have hope, until they find their destiny.

The women weren't the only ones who needed hope. I learned that night that we all had this in common. Maybe we weren't as different as I had thought. This is why I was able to fall asleep that night, with Hunter tucked in next to me. I thanked God for the day and for His gifts. I prayed that tomorrow would be even better.

Before dozing off, I came up with an idea for the next day.

After breakfast, I would call each woman into the library for a private time with me. They could tell me what their dreams were, what they hoped to accomplish, what they wanted out of my program, what they thought they needed to make it in the world. By answering these questions, they could help me figure out what I needed to do, how I could help them—because I really had no idea.

I wouldn't ask them anything about why they were sent to prison. If they wanted to tell me, fine, but I wouldn't pry. I'd let them tell me gradually—if they wanted to tell me anything at all. I also wouldn't ask them about their past relationships, unless they wanted to talk about it. My motto was "This is about having a future; let's not dwell on our mistakes."

I figured I'd start with the easiest. I'd start with the one I'd already come to love.

Tiffany.

8

Tiffany

Yesterday is history, tomorrow is a mystery,
today is a gift from God,
which is why we call it the present.

Bil Keane

As I sat across from Miss Brenda, I thought, *This is where my miracle ends.*

She looked at me all hopeful, but she had no idea what kind of terrible person I was. Once she heard my story, I was sure she'd want this filth out of her beautiful house.

So I asked her, "If I tell you the truth, are you going to make me leave?"

She smiled and said, "Of course not." Her smile seemed so loving—something I'd never seen before. Then I reminded myself that a woman who lived in a home like this had never heard a story like mine. If I told her my story, that smile would be wiped off and replaced with disgust. The miracle would end, and I'd be back to my old life. I was really liking the new life Miss Brenda was showing me, so I was determined to keep my mouth locked shut.

But before I could blink my eyes, it came gushing out of me. I'm not sure why. Maybe it was because she told me that she believed God had called her to help me. Maybe it was because I believed that inside us all is a tiny spark of hope. We get broken down by life, but that spark is still there.

I could feel it burning inside me and getting bigger as Miss Brenda smiled at me.

I was twenty-five, I told her, from Dothan, a small city in the southeastern corner of Alabama. It's the peanut capital of the world.

As long as I could remember, I was called Oreo by kids and even adults who wanted to be cruel. My mom is white and my daddy is black, so I am in between—light-skinned black with hazel eyes. To make matters worse, I have Afro hair that no one ever taught me how to style or manage so it's just all over the place. With light skin and a big head of unmanageable Afro hair, I'm an outcast everywhere, especially in a small town in Alabama like Dothan.

My parents never married. Because my daddy was in and out of prison, I'd only seen him about fifteen times in my whole life. I have a younger brother and sister. We have different fathers but we're all biracial. My mother loved black men.

My mother also loved drugs. So did my daddy. My mother's friends used to laugh about how I learned to crawl around the floor to look for my daddy's crack rock. He'd smoke crack and get so high he'd think he dropped it on the floor.

Those are my childhood memories. I also remember drug dealers coming and going in and out of our house. Even as a young child, I recognized that these were the people with money and power. And the drug addicts? They were just pitiful. I vowed that I would become a dealer and never use. I didn't want to be like my parents. But not having drugs in my life never occurred to me. Some kids dream about being doctors or lawyers. My dream was to become a big-time drug dealer.

I loved to sing and I loved to write. I put my all into my writing. I'd stand in front of the class and read my stories to everyone, and for a few minutes I'd forget. But then I'd be back in the classroom with the kids staring at me, the girl with the light skin and big crazy Afro. And I'd remember who I really was.

Oreo.

I hated school. I was bullied before being bullied was talked about so much. Besides looking different, I had almost no clothes. I wore the same outfit every day. My mom just did not seem to know how to wash anything. She bleached everything I wore. So the few clothes I had looked ridiculous. Getting high was always my mom's priority. Food, clothes, school—all were far down on the list. At night I would cry myself to sleep and pray that I would wake up and find myself in a different life, with parents who took care of me. I would be pretty, and I would be either black or white—I didn't care which, just not both.

But the morning would come and I'd still be Oreo.

My mother had a lot of boyfriends. They moved in and out very quickly. I have wondered that if I had had a father figure in my life, could life have been different? Maybe that's what I was searching for when I did the things I did—a father's love. Sometimes the men were really mean to my mother. They beat her so badly, and I would hurt for her. One time a man hit my mother so hard in the stomach that blood flew out of her mouth. I thought he had killed her.

When I was eight years old, my mom took a job working nights in a factory. We were getting our life together, she told us. She left us with Betty, a baby-sitter. One night while I was sleeping, Betty got me out of bed. She took me into the room she was staying in and had sex with a man in front of me. I had never seen anything like that before. The next night she did oral sex on me. She'd rent pornography, and I'd watch it with her. Even though I was a little girl, I knew that my life would never be the same. Feelings woke up in my body that I didn't understand, and they never went to sleep again.

My mother's plan to get our life together didn't work. She was still getting high all the time. We were always moving and getting evicted, moving and getting evicted. By the time I was thirteen, we had lived in twenty houses.

I started sneaking boys in every night while my mom was drugged out.

Some were not boys, but men. My parents always did drugs or were in prison, and I craved love and attention. I'd never had real love, but I felt as if I had found it with these men or these boys. They might not love me in the morning, but they loved me at night.

When I was thirteen I found out I was pregnant. At fourteen, I had a baby girl. I really tried to be a mom to my newborn, but I didn't know what I was doing. I would cry harder than the baby. A few months later, I was pregnant again. Both of my baby girls went to live with my grandmother—my mother's mom.

At sixteen, I achieved my dream of becoming a drug dealer. I sold crack and was a natural at it. And soon, everyone liked me. I had money; I even had clothes.

One day I felt like I needed a little boost. I was so tired. Most of my business was after two in the morning. That's when people run out of crack but want to keep on going. I had vowed never to smoke crack, but I decided that day I would smoke a little. Just this one time.

Until that day, I'd sold crack but only used powder cocaine. Crack was low-class to me. Cocaine was high-class. Crack had destroyed my parents' lives, and I wasn't going to let that happen to me.

But that night I had no coke, so I hit the crack pipe. And the minute I did, I thought, *Why in the world have I been wasting my money on powder when I could be using this wonderful stuff?* I loved it and couldn't get enough. It kept me going. I didn't eat, so I lost weight. It seemed to solve many of my problems.

I became a crack whore. Soon I was walking the streets barely dressed, jumping in and out of cars day and night. I would walk up to men and say, "I'll do something strange for some change." I won't even tell you the things I did, but I will say that there are some sick people in the world. I was the town whore. I knew that's what they called me, and I didn't mind the title. All the cops knew me. I had sex with many of them.

I was arrested all the time—for prostitution, drugs, stealing. I didn't have a rap sheet. I had rap sheets. Everyone in our town avoided me. Right before I went to prison for my first time, I had my third baby girl. I was eighteen years old. And I got high the whole time I was pregnant. I would pray that my baby would be okay as I was getting high. I know that sounds crazy, but that's what I did. I was lucky—my baby came out fine. Then I handed her over to my grandmother.

I was released after a year. A few hours later, I was high and back on the street. I would pass the house where my babies lived, and they would run to the sidewalk and cry for me. I would cross the street and wave to them. I didn't know it then, but I had become just like my parents—I didn't care about anything but getting high.

And that's how I lived. But you can only stay shot out for so long. *Shot out* is street talk for "so messed up you don't know if you're coming or going." Soon I knew where I was going—north, back to Tutwiler. I had tried to sell crack to an undercover cop. I guess I was not a very smart criminal.

The judge gave me twenty years. When she sentenced me, she said I was destined for a life in and out of prison, but mostly in. She said there was no hope for me.

And I knew she was right.

I didn't mind. I had more friends in prison than I'd ever had in my life. I felt like that was who I was. I believed the words the judge had said to me. I was destined to be in prison. This was where I belonged.

After serving just over a year, I was asked to participate in a new program called Second Chance. Of course I would go. When you're looking at twenty years, you don't hesitate to go anywhere. "Sign me up," I said. One day, the guards came and got me and said I was heading to the Lovelady Whole Way House.

On the van ride to the Lovelady house, I recognized Shay from prison. Shay was one mad black woman who had always scared me. She was so mean, so angry. No one liked her. But there was something else about Shay. She knew stuff about me that I wasn't willing to face. I don't know how she did it, but she seemed to know the truth about you, even if you didn't even know it yourself. It's like she looked at you and could see your thoughts.

And what was I thinking as I sat in the room with Miss Brenda? I was thinking that Miss Brenda might be crazy—why would anyone let people like us into her home? I was thinking that I might be part of a miracle. I was thinking that maybe I was already dead and had entered heaven when I walked into that house. I was thinking that I would do whatever I could to make sure I stayed.

I was also thinking, *I bet they have some real good crack in Birmingham.*

9

Everybody Knows

So your God is happy with you.

ISAIAH 62:5

"They know."

"They do not know."

"Do too."

We were at a Mexican restaurant near my home, having the same conversation we'd had dozens of times since the women had arrived a few days ago. We'd had it at the dentist's office where I'd taken them to get their teeth fixed. We'd had it at the doctor's office where I'd taken them for physicals. We'd had it at the grocery store, Walmart, and church. These women were convinced that everyone could tell they'd just been released from Tutwiler.

Jeff had come into town for the weekend from Gulf Shores, and we decided to take some of the women out to a restaurant. The others were with family members whom they had not seen outside of prison for many, many years. I felt the ones left behind—Tiffany, Shay, Melissa, and Parthina—needed something special to do that night so they wouldn't feel left out.

Tiffany had never been to a restaurant before—except to fly in for a quick drug deal and leave. Shay, Parthina, and Melissa had never been to a restaurant sober.

None had ever been to a Mexican restaurant before.

They were so excited they spent half the day getting ready. When they came downstairs, they had more makeup on than clothes. I could barely recognize them. "Y'all look like you're still working the streets," I said. "Take off about three-quarters of that makeup and put a safety shirt under that thing you call a blouse," I told them. "You can't whore it up anymore. Those days are over, girls."

I had a big walk-in closet and told them to choose whatever outfit they wanted. I had more clothes than I could ever wear. Plus, over the years, I'd been every size imaginable, so I had something to fit everyone—except for little Quincey, who weighed eighty pounds, but she had made plans that night with her family.

The women loved my closet. Shay dove right in, trying to beat everyone for the best outfits. Melissa was excited that she was the only one with the same size ten feet as me. "I just wished you wore heels," she told me.

Frontera Grill was the newest, hottest restaurant in town. It was packed. We had to stand by the door for quite a while until a table was ready. After the long wait, they seated us right in the center of the brightly lit restaurant.

"Everyone is staring at us," Tiffany whispered. "Look at them." She pointed to a nearby table of people.

"Tiffany, do not point," I said. "No one is staring at us."

But how could you not be curious about our motley group? People *were* sneaking glances from behind menus. I didn't care, but everyone else did. Jeff looked at me and rolled his eyes. I could tell he thought this outing was already a disaster even though it had just begun.

Tiffany studied her menu as if deciphering a foreign language. "What is all this stuff? I don't even know how to pronounce any of it. Enchi-who?"

"Burrito?"

"Chimi-what?"

"Where I come from it's all soul food, baby," Shay said. "Hog maws and chitterlings."

I laughed. "Don't worry. I'll just order for everyone. We can share and try different things."

I ordered as many types of Mexican food as possible—fajitas, tacos, enchiladas, burritos, tamales. Then the waiter brought our drinks and some chips and salsa for the table. All the women seemed happy. Even Shay wasn't her usual angry self as she shoveled tortilla chips into her mouth.

The women dunked half-eaten chips into the salsa and crammed as much into their mouths as possible. Their arms hugged their plates as they bent their heads low and inhaled chip after chip.

Jeff stared, horrified.

"Stop double dipping," I said. "Just put your chip in the dip once. You don't want to be giving everyone your germs."

About that time Jeff stopped eating chips.

I looked around the table. This is where I was supposed to be. I didn't have the answers. I hadn't figured out anything yet. I felt like I was on a trip with my suitcase packed with no idea where I was going. It would be a wonderful trip, though. God was leading the way, and I was following.

Even Jeff was coming around. He never said he was going along with my plan—and maybe he wasn't. Actually, he never said anything more about it. Jeff was still working out of Gulf Shores, but when he was in town, he would stay with me. I knew without words what Jeff was really saying. He understood that this was important to me. And if this meant so much to me, he would be there—whether he liked it or not. The night before, I had looked up from bed and there was Jeff with a suitcase. He was back in town and ready to go to sleep next to me.

But still, I knew he didn't believe my idea would work. I knew he was trying to protect me from what he thought was an idea that was certain to fail. And as much as I wanted him with me, I knew he was being the realist—our family still needed to earn a living, and Jeff's real estate work kept him at Gulf Shores. But I hoped and prayed that he would see the potential of it. I hoped and prayed he'd eventually be part of it.

I tried to compromise at bit. I told him I would find a housemother so I could spend more time at Gulf Shores. I said that for now I needed to be there—the women needed some stability. People had come and gone from their lives so many times, and I wanted them to know I wasn't going anywhere. I wanted to establish a bit of a routine for them. I would have instructors come to the house to teach some classes.

I'd still work at the real estate and mortgage offices, but Melinda, along with trusted employees Tammy and Joy and Stephanie, helped me run the business. Stephanie, a young woman who had become like a daughter to me, was a hard worker but was growing resentful of the time and attention I was giving to the Loveladies. Still, I knew I could count on her.

I explained to Jeff that despite a rocky start, I had everything under control. The women were wonderful, God was helping me, and I was making great strides. "I know you had your doubts, but everything is working out fine," I told Jeff. "Better than I ever imagined."

I flashed Jeff a big smile.

Just then Tiffany screamed, "Something's going down! Something's going down!"

The women jumped out of their seats and dove under the table. Hunter laughed, then dove under the table too.

A hush fell over the packed restaurant.

Jeff slowly looked at me and whispered, "What are they doing, Brenda?"

"Well," I replied, "it appears they're under the table."

I gave Jeff a forced smile. Then I leaned down, peeked under the table, and hissed at the women, "What are you doing?"

"Something's going down up there," Tiffany said, her eyes wide.

"What the heck are you talking about?"

"It's crazy up there," Shay said. "I've never seen anything like it—and I've seen a lot of things."

"Didn't you see it?" Tiffany asked. "The waiters are all running around like they know something we don't. There is big trouble. One of them was carrying this plate and it was on fire."

I looked back up. A fire? Two waiters were carrying plates of sizzling fajitas. "Nothing is going down! Get up from under the flippin' table," I said.

"No, something is going down."

I took a deep breath. "Listen, Mexican restaurants are just very high-paced places. The waiters run around a lot. Sometimes they carry plates of hot, sizzling food."

I pulled my head up and looked across the restaurant. Most everyone had stopped eating and was looking at our table with the women hiding underneath.

Hunter was squealing with laughter. He thought this was some grown-up version of hide-and-seek.

Jeff sat straight and proper, looking ahead and obviously wanting to be somewhere else. Eventually, he spoke: "God in heaven, Brenda, what have you done?"

I had just about convinced Jeff that I knew what I was doing. Now this. I kept forgetting the women were so unlike any I had met before. I had to remind myself of all the things I normally took for granted that the women wouldn't know how to handle or respond to. I ducked my head under the table again. "Let's have a nice dinner now. Everything's going to be fine."

These were women who had seen it all. But they were also little children peeking at the world for the first time—and sometimes hiding from it.

My hardened criminals were cowering under a table because of a fajita!

From under the table I heard Tiffany's voice: "Is everyone staring at us up there?"

"What do you think? Of course they are," I said with a sigh. "But it's too flippin' late to care."

By now even Jeff had a slight grin on his face.

The women slowly emerged just as our food arrived.

Hunter, though, was a little harder to coax up. He didn't want the game to end. Even though he had siblings, they were all much older than he. With the women, he felt like he finally had kids to play with. And they were immediately in love with him. He reminded them of the children they never raised. They loved to hold him on their lap and squeeze him. He loved the attention. In his own special way, he had become the Lovelady mascot.

When Hunter realized the party was over, he sat back in his chair just as one of the waiters raced up to our table with our entrees. I admit I was a little disappointed when at the appearance of our flaming fajitas no one dove under the table again. This time, the women barely seemed to notice.

Already my girls were growing up.

10

Imagine

Hope is a waking dream.

ARISTOTLE

Imagine if you could not remember any time in your life when you had been happy. Imagine if you'd never been to a party or a restaurant or an amusement park or a beach. It would be your birthday, and no one would give you a present or bake you a cake or even say, "Happy birthday." You never had a Christmas tree. You didn't really know about Christmas or Easter or New Year's. You never learned how to ride a bike or swim or play catch. You didn't go to your prom or a dance or a school play or a football game.

You didn't graduate from anything.

There are no photographs chronicling the first time you crawled, walked, lost a tooth, went to school. You can't remember a time when anyone took a picture of you. It's like you never existed—except for those mug shots.

Imagine if when you were born no one wanted you. There were no birth announcements. No pink or blue balloons. No celebrations. Maybe no one bothered to name you. You were never held or tucked in or rocked to sleep or read to before bed. No one gave you a bath or changed your dirty diaper. No one taught you how to brush your teeth. No one combed your hair. No one picked you up and hugged you when you cried. No one fed you when you were hungry. No one wondered if you went to school. When you came home, no one noticed. No one washed your clothes. No one cared that you wore the same pair of underwear for weeks.

Imagine if your parents didn't protect you from evil. They were drug addicts who left you alone for days—dirty, cold, hungry, and scared. They joked about putting drugs in your bottle so you'd fall asleep and leave them to their drugs. Or they left you with strangers who abused you. When you told them about being abused by someone, they didn't do anything to stop it. Actually, they didn't care about anything except their next fix.

Imagine if when your parents ran out of drug money, they gave you to drug dealers in exchange for dope. Your parents consented to your rape. You knew it didn't seem right, but they were your parents, so you thought it was normal. The only time you felt close to your parents was when they smoked crack with you or shot up with you.

Family time was a crack pipe.

Imagine if living on the streets and turning tricks for money was a better alternative to staying home. Getting thrown in jail was something you assumed would eventually happen to you, and when it did, you were not surprised. It was a rite of passage you expected in your life. After all, everyone in your family has been to prison at one time or other. So have your friends. It is your normal. Even your family vacations were road trips to prison to visit parents or relatives.

Imagine feeling that prison is where you belong because you know of nothing else. When you get released, you may miss it there. Prison is bad, but so is the uncertainty of the street. You might test dirty on purpose just to go back and get away from the hell of the street, an abusive boyfriend, a murderous pimp, the unrelenting hunger.

Sometimes prison seems like home. You have your family—your state mama, your state sisters and state brothers. You have chow and a place to sleep. You can get drugs there. You can survive.

I had come a long way. I remembered how I'd used to see women like these and look the other way. I'd view them as crackheads, druggies, whores. In my mind I'd label them as pathetic, worthless, disgusting, disgraceful losers.

I believed they deserved to be where they were. They didn't deserve anything better. They didn't deserve a second chance.

But after just a few days now living with these women, I realized most of them had never even had a *first* chance. I realized I had to see them with my heart—not my eyes. And so I imagined, to the best of my ability, the lives they had endured.

One day I noticed a little girl sitting on a corner in a questionable part of the city. She was pretty with blond hair and blue eyes. But she looked so sad. Somehow my heart went out to her.

Some days later, a parole officer brought to my house a woman to be entered into the program. That woman, wasted and bedraggled, looked to me so much like that little girl I'd seen on the street. I knew immediately what the Lord was showing me—no one had bothered to save that woman when she was a little girl. She never had a real chance.

God calls us to the hopeless. The unlovable. The ones who aren't so cute anymore. The ones no one wants. The ones we ourselves have judged.

Suga-Suga (my nickname for Tiffany) wanted to be independent but had no idea how to do that. I knew I had to raise her as if she were a young child. So I started giving her the most basic chores—making her bed, sweeping the room, setting the table. Often people who have been abused are stunted at the age when the abuse began. In some ways, she was just a small child. In other ways, she was a worldly woman who had been used and abused by too many men to count. It was how she survived. She didn't know there was any other way.

Tiffany always had a smile for everyone. She became the woman all the others would go to when they wanted comforting. "Suga, don't cry," she'd say. While she comforted them, they also thought of her as the baby they wanted to take care of and protect. There was something so innocent and naive about Suga-Suga.

Quincey was the one they'd seek out when they were angry and wanted someone to be angry with. She could get the women riled up over nothing. Quincey was so full of anger—that's how she landed in prison. On September 26, 1996, when she was twenty-six, Quincey and a friend had gotten into a bar fight. It started as a shouting match and escalated until they were both armed with broken beer bottles. Quincey said she was defending herself as her friend charged toward her. Her bottle slashed her friend's neck and she bled to death. "I never meant for that to happen," she said. "But I have to live with the fact that I am responsible for someone's death for the rest of my life."

Quincey was convicted of manslaughter and sent to prison for twenty years. Her then young sons, Kevin and Antonio, were raised by her parents. They brought them to prison whenever Quincey was allowed visitors. Quincey tried to mother them as much as possible from her prison cell. She'd write them letters and talk to them on the phone whenever she could. After serving seven years, she wanted to be with her boys. She hated being stuck here with us. And she made sure we knew it.

Before she went to prison, Quincey had never been in any kind of trouble. You would think her imprisonment would have taught her a lesson about self-control, but she was mad at the world and always ready to explode. I began to think that it was a matter of time before her volatile temper would land her back in prison. However, I also knew there was this vulnerable side to Quincey—she loved her boys, and her eyes would fill up with tears when she talked about them. She had deep regrets that she had missed so much of their childhood.

I signed her up for anger-management classes. She had lofty goals and I knew she could accomplish them if she could control her temper. She wanted to make a lot of money, have nice cars, and own a home. She'd tell me proudly, "I did the time, but I didn't let the time do me." She took as many classes as she could while at Tutwiler. She studied computer science and became certified in cosmetology. She wanted a job where she'd be respected; she wanted to be a boss.

In time, I was able to put her to work as a receptionist at our mortgage company.

Quincey loved her daddy and talked about him constantly. It was always Daddy-this and Daddy-that. If she wasn't talking about him, Quincey was on the phone with him. The women who had no relationships with their fathers or didn't know their fathers took Quincey's comments as bragging.

"We're sick and tired of hearing about your daddy," Shay would say.

Quincey had given me so much attitude during those first few days that I was sick of her. She kept calling her daddy, crying and begging him to pick her up. "I hate it here," she'd say loud enough for all to hear.

One day we were coming back from church, heading to an elderly woman's home to help her clean and organize. "I am not a maid and I'm not going," Quincey said defiantly. "Take me back to your house."

"No," I said calmly. "We're all going to help. I'm going too."

"No," she snapped. "I'm sick of being told what to do, what to say, how to act. I did it all those years in prison, and I don't want to do it anymore. I want my life back now. I'm not going to this house."

"Yes you are."

"No I'm not. Don't think I don't know what you're doing. You're just making money off of us. You're fixing to get rich off all of us. Well, I'm not going along with your plan."

She screamed at me in her high-pitched voice while everyone else looked on with their mouths hanging open.

I slammed on the brakes. "I'm sick of your attitude, Quincey. Get out of the van now!"

Quincey gasped. "Are you crazy? You can't put me out here. We're in the middle of nowhere."

"I'll put you out if you do not apologize to me and everyone in the van right now."

"I will never apologize, and I will report you to the authorities."

"Oh, please."

The women were enjoying the show. Quincey was so angry I couldn't imagine her apologizing, and neither could the other women. But they wondered if I'd really put her out of the car and leave her in the middle of nowhere. Did I have it in me?

I knew I'd really screwed up by threatening this. It would hurt the program if it was discovered I'd put a parolee out on the street. But I couldn't back down. I'd learned already that if I was not respected according to the code by which they lived, they would never respect me or accept the code I was teaching them.

So I got out of the van and opened the sliding door, knowing the whole time I couldn't really desert her. But she had to believe I would. She had to apologize or I'd lose all credibility. *Would she see my bluff?* I angrily reached for Quincey, my heart pounding.

"Get out," I said. "I'm done with you."

Quincey looked at me, her eyes wide with fear.

I kept up my act. "Get out now!"

She just sat there. I could tell she was debating what to do.

"I'm sorry," Quincey said finally in a meek voice. "I'm sorry about my attitude."

It wasn't much of an apology, but I was eager to take what I could get. "Okay," I said. I gave her a quick hug. I got behind the wheel and slowly drove off.

As simple a confrontation as that was, right there a new Quincey was born.

Well, almost. She still had a long road of anger-management classes ahead of her. But after that time, her demeanor changed. I had proved myself to her and won her respect.

Charmain was an obsessive germophobe who was constantly cleaning—scrubbing floors, ironing her clothes (even her underwear), washing spotless glasses before she'd use them. She couldn't stand it when other women left out dirty dishes or clothes. She didn't want roommates because no one could keep up with her high standards of cleanliness. If someone left a dirty shirt on a bed, she'd have a meltdown. We'd tell her she didn't have to constantly clean, but she couldn't help herself. She was always moving around the house with a mop or a broom or a duster. It was therapy to her.

"Stop cleaning," I'd yell.

"I love cleaning—it's my nature," she explained. "I love everything feeling and smelling fresh. It clears my mind." She'd also take half-hour showers, which also drove the other women crazy. She couldn't get clean enough.

Of all the women, Charmain was the most complicated. What you saw was not what you got. She was funny, yet extremely serious. She was bright but acted as if she wasn't. She loved her seven-year-old son but was afraid to raise him. She acted cool and confident but had no self-esteem. She pretended she didn't need anyone, yet she was always trying to please everyone.

In some ways, I understood Charmain better than all the other women. We shared a similar addiction—money.

Charmain had lived in Huntsville, a wealthier Alabama city, where she had built a successful career selling drugs. It was a family business that her cousins introduced her to when she was fifteen. She saw how well they lived and she wanted to be part of it. They taught her the ropes. She loved making money and loved all its perks—the expensive clothes, watches, cars. I had a mink coat that I no longer wore; Charmain loved putting it on and looking at herself in the mirror.

When I asked her about her past, she would proudly say, "I was a dope slanger." Drug dealer. Her past ran deep and wide inside her veins and it frightened me. I wanted Charmain to learn she could have a successful career that had nothing to do with drugs. Charmain was twenty-eight and had spent half her life in the family business. Was she just passing time here until she could get back in the business? Was I really accomplishing anything with her?

"The money you made selling drugs wasn't really your money," I said. "You always had to worry about it being taken away from you by another criminal or the police. But you can do something positive and work hard and make money that is really yours."

Charmain believed that living in the house with me was her destiny. She became convinced I was somehow her long-lost mother. I'd have to tuck her into bed so tight that the blankets were taut against her. Once she was tucked in, she'd stay that way all night, even if she had to use the bathroom. She didn't want to undo that tuck-in. It was as if my tuck-in had magical power.

When other women imitated Charmain and called me Mama, she became furious. She said, "Y'all can call her Mama, and I won't stop you, but she's going to be Mommy to me. And you can't ever call her that."

So Mommy became the sacred title that no one could use for me except Charmain and Hunter. It drove my other children crazy. "You're not her mommy," Beau and Matthew would say. "And you're not their mama. You're our mama!"

Parthina was the invisible one. She would be in a room, sitting in a chair, and it was like she wasn't there. Miss Cellophane. She'd sit on the outskirts, listening or pretending to listen. She did what she was supposed to, but sometimes it seemed she was just going through the motions. I'd ask her a question, and she wouldn't look up. I couldn't figure her out. Did she want to change? Was she just biding time? I wanted so desperately to help her.

Suzanne, on the other hand, blew in and immediately began to make plans to blow out. She had her family's support, which made all the difference. When your family is there for you, it's much easier to attain your goals. And I knew she'd attain her goals.

Within the first hours of her arrival, Suzanne's beautiful, well-dressed preacher mother showed up with a cell phone and Bluetooth. She gave Suzanne cell phone lessons and stuck the Bluetooth in her ear, and in a matter of minutes, Suzanne was strolling throughout the house talking and laughing on her phone. The other women were so jealous, yet their jealousy was less about the actual phone and more about the fact that even if they did have a phone, they had no one to call.

I sat down with Suzanne and explained that I was not going to allow her to be on the phone around the house.

We called Suzanne "the Queen" because she wouldn't do any of her chores.

"She thinks her poop don't stink," Shay said.

Suzanne went to prison when she was eighteen and had been there for eight years. Suzanne was determined to succeed and make something of her life. She'd been in a car with her brother during a drive-by shooting in front of a high school football game. She served eight years as an accessory to the crime. The system had failed her, she felt, and she didn't believe she should have served any time. Her brother is serving a life sentence for murder without the chance of parole.

She didn't understand why she had been sentenced. She believed she was a victim of circumstance. She just happened to be in a car when a kid got shot, so she shouldn't have been punished at all. Suzanne never accepted her guilt and felt like she was better than the other women. She rid herself of Tutwiler as if it were dog crap on her shoe. She wiped it off and forgot about it immediately.

She seemed certain she would make something of her life and talked about applying to nursing school. I wasn't worried about her. She had more skills than most of these women had. She knew how to eat, how to talk, how to act in the free world.

Whereas Suzanne was brimming with self-esteem, Melissa had none. She had been in and out of treatment centers in addition to prisons, but she couldn't break her addiction to cocaine. "I want to be self-sufficient and a better mother to my three kids, but I don't know how," she said.

Melissa was so pretty that the women compared her to Vanessa Williams and Beyoncé. When I spoke to her, she told me she believed hope was for other people. I asked what she wanted to accomplish. She couldn't answer me. "I don't even know how to dream," she said.

Melissa's childhood had been filled with incest and abuse. She had been raised by her mother and a stepfather who hated her. She never knew her biological father. As a child, she'd been molested by her uncle. When she was in high school, she felt like she was finally healing and moving past her abuse. She excelled in sports and her studies and was happy there.

She still remembers the day she made the school's basketball team. She ran over to the list where the coach had written all the girls' names. Her name was on the top—the best. Maybe her life would turn out okay, she thought. But was it normal for a fifteen-year-old girl to be tired all the time? A few days later, she learned she had leukemia and would probably die.

Melissa went through chemo and survived. During her treatments, she stopped going to school and never went back. When she was free of her disease, she had no plans and no skills. She was supposed to be dead. Instead, she had nowhere to go. She became addicted to drugs. I knew Melissa wanted to change, but she felt hopeless and afraid. I also knew she had had problems with men—she'd been in and out of too many bad relationships.

And Shay, the angry woman no one liked, needed more help than all of them combined. I found myself drawn to her, and I wracked my brain trying to figure out a way to reach her. If I couldn't get through to her, she was destined to return to prison. She'd been in and out of it for most of her life.

Unless I helped her change, I didn't think there was much hope for her or for this program. If I couldn't help the toughest, most lost cause, then this all might be a failure.

Shay had been so deeply hurt by life and had so much hatred in her heart. I wasn't sure what had happened to her—she wouldn't let me in. Even as we sat on the couch during a private meeting, she sat as far away from me as possible. She didn't trust me. She didn't believe I would be there for the duration. Shay's whole life had been comprised of so many broken promises. Why would this be different?

Would I be different?

"For God's sake, get closer," I said when she and I were talking one-on-one in the library. Shay wouldn't budge. She seemed to squirm a little farther away from me on the couch.

"I'm not going to open up my dirty closet," she snapped.

"Not asking you to. I want to help you change your life so you don't go back to prison."

Shay narrowed her eyes. "I know what you want. You want me to give you all my garbage, tell you all my secrets. I've done it before. I don't want to go through that again."

"Good golly, Shay. I do not need to know anything about your past. We're dealing with the future now. I just want to know what you want to become. What you want me to help you accomplish while you're staying here. I want to help you, Shay."

Shay huffed. Would she answer my question or was she angry with me—again?

She let out a long sigh. "Lady, I don't know how to live. I don't know how to be normal. I know the type of person I want to be. I want to be a good person. I've tried before, and I couldn't do it. I just don't know how."

I nodded. Shay looked at me for an answer, but I didn't know what to say. Out of all the women in the house, Shay was smart enough to figure out that I really didn't know what I was doing. Had she discovered my secret yet? How could I help Shay when all of this was new to me?

I understood that Shay needed to be a leader. If she could lead, maybe she could flourish. I also realized that if I could flip her authority around and make her lead for me rather than against me, I just might make this work—for her and the program.

All the women listened to Shay. Most of them couldn't stand her, but still for some reason they listened to her.

"Well, we'll figure this all out together," I said. "But for now, I need your help."

Shay eyed me as if she wasn't sure where this was heading. Was I going to finally disappoint her with a list of demands?

"You're going to be a mini-housemom."

Shay's face instantly lit up. "You mean I get to tell everyone what to do? I get to be their boss?"

I laughed. "Not like that. You're not going to boss them. We're going to let them figure it out. But I need you to help me run this place. I'll give you the keys to the house and the alarm code for when I'm not here and—"

"You're giving me the keys to your house?" Shay looked shocked. "And the code to your alarm?"

I nodded.

"Most people have alarms to keep people like me out."

I smiled. "I know."

For once Shay was speechless.

"Another thing…"

"Yeah?"

"Well, since the cook quit on account of you, I need someone who can cook. From what I hear, you were a cook in prison. Can you cook for us?"

"'Course I can cook. I watched my mom cook, and she could make a meal out of nothing. Yes ma'am, I can cook."

It's funny how life works sometimes. Shay came to my house furious that I was going to give her a maid's outfit and an endless list of chores. A few days later she was the house cook, and she seemed very happy in the role.

Her first few meals had us terrified, and we took hesitant bites, convinced she might poison us all.

But soon Hob Hill was filled with the aromas of authentic southern cooking—some scents I'd never smelled before. And Shay, whose face had seemed etched in a permanent scowl, would occasionally smile as she stirred a pot or sprinkled ingredients or headed to the walk-in pantry.

Of course she only smiled when she thought no one was looking.

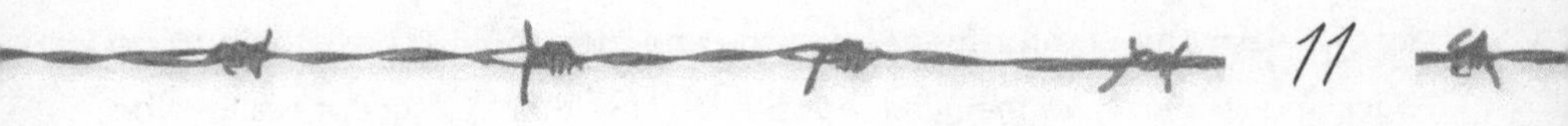

11

Shay

A man cannot be comfortable
without his own approval.

MARK TWAIN

I was comfortable in prison. I knew what to expect. There were no surprises and no disappointments. There were no false promises. It was exactly what it was supposed to be—horrible, miserable, degrading, humiliating. I could work that world because I knew how to hustle. I was confident in that world.

I was big stuff there.

I understood that this crazy lady wanted me to talk. She wanted me to welcome her into my dirty closet, but I didn't even know where to begin. I had no idea how to have a conversation in the free world without hustling, conning, and lying. I put up a block on who I really was and what I've been through.

She told me that God loves me. I didn't say anything. I thought to myself that this broad was just about the craziest person I'd ever met—and I've met a lot of crazies. God may love her, but He skipped over me. Big-time. He didn't care anything about me, and I didn't want Him to. I wanted to tell Crazy Lady that if there really was a God, why didn't He help me when I was a little girl—before I was ruined?

What do I want to be? I want to be a good person—but what do I do to become that person? I want to be a mother to my children, but how can

I be? I wasn't around for them when they needed me. Do I ask them to go back and let me relive their childhoods? Do I ask them to accept me for who I am at this moment? Do I ask them to get past the past?

I didn't love them when they were little. I didn't love anyone when I was on drugs. It was all about the drugs and nothing else. But I don't even know how to say this aloud. How do I get them to not look at the past pains I caused and know that I love them today? Could they see me as something more than a crackhead? Could I still somehow be their mother?

I didn't say any of this to Crazy Lady. And then out of nowhere, she asked me to help her, to be the cook. It was like she saw something in me I hadn't figured out yet. I always felt in my heart that I could cook. But I had no idea how she could see into my heart.

"Can you cook, sweetie?" she asked.

I knew the cook had quit on account of my badass attitude. And I thought, *Bring it on.*

I was so angry a few days earlier when I was convinced Crazy Lady wanted us to be her maids. If she had asked me to cook then, I would have yelled and cussed and carried on. I would have told the other women, "See, I was right." But this lady was doing everything we were doing. I didn't know they made people like her and her daughter. She'd cook and clean and make beds and wash clothes. Of course she always had Tiffany, her favorite, with her.

Tiffany didn't know how to do one thing. Crazy Lady was leading her by the hand as if she were a small child, which she was. Tiffany was my baby girl. She showed Tiffany how to wash clothes. One time, I saw Tiffany pour bleach into a load of darks. I knew my clothes were mixed in there, and I didn't care. I was so excited to see a major breakdown and show everyone that Miss Do-Gooder wasn't all about peace, hope, and love. As soon as the buzzer went off, I said ever so casually, "Tif, your clothes are ready for the dryer." She and Miss Brenda headed toward the laundry room. I thought, Miss Crazy Do-Gooder's gonna kill her. Then the door opened. Tiffany was crying, but Crazy Lady hugged her and said that the towels looked fine all spotted.

"It adds a little spice to life," Crazy said, hugging her little pet.

I couldn't believe it.

But to cook in that beautiful kitchen with the big center island! I would shut the door to the pantry. Every time I went in there, I was in awe. It was a room bigger than my bedroom growing up. I couldn't believe this woman had all this stuff—or that she was so carefree about it. She'd just say, "Fix whatever you want." All my life I was used to hearing, "Put that back." Everything had always been limited, but with her, nothing was limited. We could take anything. And everything I thought my taste buds could ever desire when I was in prison was in that room. There were all kinds of spices, seasonings, sauces, broths, stocks. That room was my favorite spot in the house. I'd go in there to be alone and read recipes. The other women liked to go in there and stare too, but I told 'em to keep out. I was the cook and they were getting in my way. It was my pantry. I'd give them my angry face and they'd run out.

There would be no pasta or any Italian dishes as long as I was the chef. I'm from Mobile, where we love cooking soul food. I guess I just knew how to cook from watching my mom. My mom's cooking always brought a lot of people and love to the table. I wanted to be able to do that too. I'd cook up fried chicken and corn bread, grits, chitterlings with hog maws, ham hocks, neck bones, and lots and lots of beans.

They finally said to me, "No more beans."

My favorite meal was seafood gumbo. I'd put everything in it—crabs, crawfish, shrimp, okra, onions, and red pepper. Then I'd set it all out on the center island and watch the ladies fix a plate and eat.

Of course I figured the ex-cons would love it—they were used to eating prison chow. But Brenda's family loved it too, so I knew I was doing good—even though they knew nothing about soul food. One time, Melinda came into the kitchen and dipped a spoon into a pot to taste what I was cooking.

"Delicious, sweetie. What is it?"

"Chitterlings and hog maws."

Poor Melinda just about turned white as a ghost and began gagging. I thought she was going to throw up.

"What? I just ate hog balls?"

"Not hog balls. Hog maws."

"What?"

"Hog maws." I laughed harder than I had in a long time. Then I explained to poor Melinda that hog maw is pig stomach.

I don't think that made her feel much better.

After that, no one in Miss Brenda's family ate soul food without asking exactly what was in it first. Come to think of it, I don't believe Miss Brenda touched much of it.

Some of the women saw I had all this responsibility and figured I was more important than the average Lovelady. Some called me Miss Shay.

Miss Shay!

No one had ever called me that before. I'd cook and they'd sit at the center island, and some would start telling me what they were going through. And I realized I was actually helping them as I was cooking. I guess that's what happens when you are the chef. People will talk and talk and think you're helping them when really all you're doing is preparing a meal and listening.

If Miss Brenda wasn't around, I'd set the alarm to her beautiful mansion. I'd never lived anywhere that had an alarm system except prison, but that doesn't count. I'd say, "Okay, ladies, it's time for bed." Then I'd set the code. Imagine giving me—AIS number 118074—the code to an alarm to keep out the bad guys? I was big stuff.

I thought, *Man, so much is happening at once. So much is changing.* I wanted to believe this was really happening, but I was scared. I was prepared to be disappointed. It was too good to be true. I never dreamed my life could be like this.

So I was positive it wouldn't last.

12

The Lord's Prayer

Do not be like them, for your Father knows what you need before you ask him. This, then, is how you should pray: "Our Father in heaven..."

MATTHEW 6:8–9

"In the library!" That was my code to the women. It meant I'd come up with an idea for a class. I'd just started doing this. Seems like every day I'd have a new idea. There was so much they didn't know about the free world and so much I didn't know about their world.

So when I'd yell, "In the library!" the women would stop what they were doing and meet me there; they'd bring their Bible, a notebook, and a pen.

Today I led by saying, "We're gonna learn to pray."

I believe faith is the most important part of rehabilitation. I believe that without faith, these women were doomed to wind up back in prison. Faith is what separated the Lovelady Whole Way House from all the other transitional programs.

I had spoken to the women about God's love, but were they really listening? Did they believe in God, or were they pretending so they could stay in the program and bide their time until they could leave?

"I don't need to learn to pray. I already know how to pray," Quincey said with her usual attitude.

I gave her a look. *Will you shut up and listen for once!*

"Do y'all pray to God?" I asked them.

"Why would I pray to God? Where was He when I needed Him?"

It was a sentiment most of the women shared. Why would they pray to a God they felt had abandoned them through most of their lives? Why hadn't God protected them from rape, abuse, pain, and suffering? How could a loving God allow such atrocities to happen to them, especially when they were little children? How could God create abusive men or drug-addicted parents?

If such evil existed, how could there be a God?

"It's something we've all struggled with," I said. "Even me."

I told them a story from my childhood. When I was thirteen, a young girl in Tennessee was killed by her abusive stepfather. For weeks, it was all the adults discussed. I overheard my parents and their friends speaking of the atrocity in hushed voices. Being who I was, I got caught up in it, listening to my parents' conversation and absorbing every sordid detail. I couldn't believe that evil like this existed. The little girl was forced to eat hot sauce and cayenne pepper with nothing to drink. Scalding water was poured over her by her daddy, and her entire body was burned. She suffered from severe malnutrition.

I became consumed by this story. I became so angry at God for allowing this to happen to a little girl like me. After a month, I had worked myself into such a frenzy that I couldn't sleep. My mother and daddy didn't know what to do, so they took me to speak to the pastor at our church.

Pastor Bob Gaultney was such a wonderful man. I loved him so much. No matter what I needed to know, he would stay with me until I understood.

So I tried to think about what my former pastor would say as these women struggled with the same questions. How could God be with them when they had been so abused by life?

I explained to them that one of the gifts God bestowed upon us is free will. Every human has volition—the highest power of choice. And many times innocent people are adversely affected by the volition of others. It is a very sad thing, but that is the simple truth.

"We all look to blame God," I said. "We don't want to take things as they are, so who can we blame but God? But it's not God's fault. God didn't abandon you. He is always there for you. And He's here with us right now. I believe we are together, here, because of His plan for all of us. I prayed to Him to send me women to help. I believe He chose each of you to be here."

I told them that if they would pray, they could begin to have a relationship with God. I told them we'd start with the Lord's Prayer. "That's what Jesus taught people to pray. If it's good enough for Jesus, it's good enough for us."

The women all knew the Lord's Prayer. Most had said it many times before, but did they really know what they were reciting? After a while, prayers become mechanical. When we say prayers without really hearing them, the words become devoid of meaning. I know because I've done it myself.

"If you really listen to the words, you will see how beautiful and simple they are—and how the prayer covers everything you will ever need. You shouldn't think of prayer as something hard and complicated. Praying is just talking to God. Once you start praying regularly, you'll feel like you have a real relationship with God. Once you have a real relationship with God, you can get through anything."

And so we began…

Our Father in heaven.

"You are recognizing God as your Father," I explained.

Hallowed be Your name.

"God, You're so awesome. You're so great."

Your kingdom come.

I paraphrased: "This is the most important part. You're praying for the Lord to use you as His kingdom on earth. Make Him Lord of your life, just like He is in heaven."

Your will be done on earth as it is in heaven.

"This is what we want to happen. We can make requests to God, but we have to trust in His will. We have to trust that God knows what is best for us, even if it might not seem that way at times."

Give us this day our daily bread.

"Many people think this is just about food, but it isn't. You're asking for your needs to be met, whatever they are."

And forgive us our debts, as we forgive our debtors.

"This is where it gets really important and really hard. At times this seems impossible. You're asking God to forgive your sins to the same degree as you forgive those who sin against you. So if you don't forgive someone the whole way, you're asking God to forgive you only part of the way too. You're asking to be forgiven to the same measure as you forgive others."

And do not lead us into temptation, but deliver us from the evil one.

"Help us to not sin."

For Yours is the kingdom and the power and the glory forever.

"You are the greatest. I love You."

The women nodded their heads. They understood.

"But God doesn't want you to say just this prayer. You can personalize it with your requests. You can ask for whatever you want."

"How about to help me budget my money better?" asked Tiffany, who was finally making money but could not save a penny.

"That's right," I said.

"Help me with my anger problems," said Quincey, who was in yet another anger management class.

"Yes."

"Help me pass my driver's test," said Shay, who'd been driving forever but was studying to finally get her license.

"Now you're getting it... And please, Lord, help me help all these women live wonderful, beautiful, amazing lives."

Amen.

13

Tiffany

Housekeeping ain't no joke.

LOUISA MAY ALCOTT

I told Miss Brenda my goals: I wanted to be independent, I wanted to have my own home one day, I wanted my girls in my life. I felt so bad that I hadn't been a mother to them just like my mother hadn't been a mother to me.

I didn't know how to be a mother. I didn't know how to be anything except high.

I never cleaned. I never cooked. I hated living that way, but I didn't even know I hated it until I saw how organized, how clean, how neat Miss Brenda's house was. I wanted to live just like her. I didn't have to live in a big mansion like Miss Brenda's, but I wanted to have a nice, neat place of my own one day.

I had never made a bed before, except for that cot in the prison. But not a real bed with sheets and blankets and quilts and a bunch of pillows. I'd just leave it unmade.

"Suga-Suga," Miss Brenda would say, "you want to live nice, so you have to make your bed." I'd put the quilt over my messy sheets. Miss Brenda would pull it apart and show me how to do it. Tucking this in and that in. I had never dusted or vacuumed or mopped. I know it sounds like easy things to do, but imagine the first time a child does these things. They don't do a very good job. But at least that child is trying her best to imitate how her mama does it. As a child, I didn't have anyone to imitate. My mama lived in filth.

I had to learn that you don't just push a mop over the floor without dunking it in fresh water and cleaner. You don't throw all different colored laundry into the washing machine. You don't dump bleach into the wash. I ruined a lot of clothes that way. I thought Miss Brenda might just finally go crazy and say, "Okay, Tiffany, find somewhere else to live." But she never did.

We all were given jobs with a salary. Some of the women left the house and worked at Miss Brenda's businesses. But I stayed at the house with Miss Brenda, learning how to do everything. I think some of the other women were jealous that I got to spend so much time with Miss Brenda. Shay would give me her mean face, but I'd pretend I didn't see it. I was so happy to spend time with Miss Brenda. I would dust the entire house. I would vacuum, sweep, and mop. I had no idea so much went into keeping a house clean. When I started, I'd wash the top of a counter and think I was done, but Miss Brenda was a neat freak. I had to dust underneath things. I even dusted the indoor plants. I dusted the baseboards and vents. It was a lot of work, but I loved it. I'd sing songs by my favorite singer—Mary J. Blige—and concentrate on whatever I was doing. I felt like I was really accomplishing something.

I felt so happy.

I loved shopping with Miss Brenda for cleaning products—Murphy's Oil for the furniture, Bona for the hardwood floors, Comet for the bathrooms. I loved the smell of it all—eucalyptus, bleach, lemon. My favorite was OdoBan, the cleaning disinfectant. One time I stood in Walmart for a half hour trying to decide if I liked the freesia or the lavender scent better. Until Miss Brenda, I never went shopping for anything unless I was high. Until Miss Brenda, I never knew things could smell so good.

Since her nanny also quit on account of us being so scary, Miss Brenda asked me to watch Hunter. I knew nothing about taking care of a little boy

13

Tiffany

Housekeeping ain't no joke.

LOUISA MAY ALCOTT

I told Miss Brenda my goals: I wanted to be independent, I wanted to have my own home one day, I wanted my girls in my life. I felt so bad that I hadn't been a mother to them just like my mother hadn't been a mother to me.

I didn't know how to be a mother. I didn't know how to be anything except high.

I never cleaned. I never cooked. I hated living that way, but I didn't even know I hated it until I saw how organized, how clean, how neat Miss Brenda's house was. I wanted to live just like her. I didn't have to live in a big mansion like Miss Brenda's, but I wanted to have a nice, neat place of my own one day.

I had never made a bed before, except for that cot in the prison. But not a real bed with sheets and blankets and quilts and a bunch of pillows. I'd just leave it unmade.

"Suga-Suga," Miss Brenda would say, "you want to live nice, so you have to make your bed." I'd put the quilt over my messy sheets. Miss Brenda would pull it apart and show me how to do it. Tucking this in and that in. I had never dusted or vacuumed or mopped. I know it sounds like easy things to do, but imagine the first time a child does these things. They don't do a very good job. But at least that child is trying her best to imitate how her mama does it. As a child, I didn't have anyone to imitate. My mama lived in filth.

I had to learn that you don't just push a mop over the floor without dunking it in fresh water and cleaner. You don't throw all different colored laundry into the washing machine. You don't dump bleach into the wash. I ruined a lot of clothes that way. I thought Miss Brenda might just finally go crazy and say, "Okay, Tiffany, find somewhere else to live." But she never did.

We all were given jobs with a salary. Some of the women left the house and worked at Miss Brenda's businesses. But I stayed at the house with Miss Brenda, learning how to do everything. I think some of the other women were jealous that I got to spend so much time with Miss Brenda. Shay would give me her mean face, but I'd pretend I didn't see it. I was so happy to spend time with Miss Brenda. I would dust the entire house. I would vacuum, sweep, and mop. I had no idea so much went into keeping a house clean. When I started, I'd wash the top of a counter and think I was done, but Miss Brenda was a neat freak. I had to dust underneath things. I even dusted the indoor plants. I dusted the baseboards and vents. It was a lot of work, but I loved it. I'd sing songs by my favorite singer—Mary J. Blige—and concentrate on whatever I was doing. I felt like I was really accomplishing something.

I felt so happy.

I loved shopping with Miss Brenda for cleaning products—Murphy's Oil for the furniture, Bona for the hardwood floors, Comet for the bathrooms. I loved the smell of it all—eucalyptus, bleach, lemon. My favorite was Odo-Ban, the cleaning disinfectant. One time I stood in Walmart for a half hour trying to decide if I liked the freesia or the lavender scent better. Until Miss Brenda, I never went shopping for anything unless I was high. Until Miss Brenda, I never knew things could smell so good.

Since her nanny also quit on account of us being so scary, Miss Brenda asked me to watch Hunter. I knew nothing about taking care of a little boy and couldn't believe she trusted me with her son. I guess Miss Brenda was teaching me how to be a mother with her own child since I couldn't be a mother to my children. Hunter and me weren't that much different. I was a big kid who was ready to have a childhood.

I'd tell Miss Brenda that Hunter wanted to go to Chuck E. Cheese's, or the playground, or Disney On Ice, or the amusement park.

She'd look at me and say, "Does Hunter want to go or do you?"

I'd tell her it was Hunter. Why would a grown woman want to go to Chuck E. Cheese's?

But it was me. I loved playing Whac-a-Mole.

14

"In the Library!"

The best way to find out if you
can trust somebody is to trust them.

ERNEST HEMINGWAY

It was getting close to Thanksgiving—the first time many of the Loveladies were allowed to go on extended passes to visit their families. They were scared. So was I. In the past few weeks we'd accomplished so much and settled into a comfortable routine. But would all this progress be erased during a four-day pass?

Yes, according to the statistics. The first visit back home is the toughest because it is easy to fall into old behaviors and surrender to temptations. Many programs do not offer passes to newly released prisoners so early in the rehabilitation process. When the parole officers asked me what I wanted to do, my first thought was, *I can't let these women go. That's crazy.* But I believed if I didn't give them the freedom to leave, then our program would be no different from all the other places that keep their residents locked up as if they're still in prison. The women had to know I trusted them. They also had to learn how to become part of society.

But could I really trust them not to relapse? not to commit crimes? not to disappear forever?

I wasn't sure.

No one could understand why our program was working. The parole officers were shocked I hadn't called them to report crimes, relapses, or problems. I didn't understand it either, but I knew this: I was the first person ever to trust these women without asking them to earn my trust first. Shortly after they arrived, I had said to them, "The minute you walked through my door, you received a clean bill of health. You are a newborn person with no past, nothing. Until you show me you cannot be trusted, I trust you."

And the women began trusting me.

When they had first arrived, their biggest fear was that I would send them away. They had been rejected all their lives, so they assumed I'd eventually reject them too. I assured them this wouldn't happen unless they broke the law. They didn't believe me. They were afraid if they made me mad, I'd kick them out. They were so careful around me. They'd whisper to each other: "Don't tell her you broke that." "Don't you dare show her what you did." I always heard them—they didn't whisper well.

I discovered that Tiffany had broken some knickknacks while cleaning the house.

I learned that Shay was charging some of the women for extra food.

"What? Are you kidding me? You can't charge the women for extra food. It's *my* food."

Shay didn't understand why I was annoyed with her.

"That's how we do it in prison. It's the code. Two-for-one. If someone gives you something, you have to give them two back."

"How many times do I have to tell you? You're not in prison anymore."

I asked Tiffany to be more careful. I asked Shay to stop her two-for-ones. But I didn't tell them to leave.

The women weren't the only ones making mistakes. I was making plenty too. I learned I was too impatient with them. I thought I could solve their problems by helping them forget about their past and concentrate on their future. I would rush them through their stories of pain and abuse as if the pain no longer mattered.

"That's in the past. Don't worry about it," I would say. "Let it go."

One day, Tiffany looked up at me, her hazel eyes brimming with pain. In a quiet voice she said, "I can't just let it go."

I had failed to see how important it was for these women to talk. After that, I would remind myself to take time every single day to sit down and listen to them for as long as they needed my ear. Until these women arrived, I hadn't realized what a bad listener I'd been all my life—to my family, my employees, my friends. I had to learn to quiet my mind and my big mouth.

The women taught me how to listen.

It was when I really heard them that they began to trust me.

We had established some routines. They were sleeping in a little later, getting up at six instead of four in the morning. They still turned on every light at bedtime. I'd still turn every light off. Sometime after I fell asleep, they'd turn the lights back on.

Charmain, who was petrified of the dark, had me tuck her in every night. I'd have to tell her a story about my childhood and treat her like a little girl. "You're my mommy," she'd say. She had been one of seven children and needed so much love, but with all those siblings, she never felt her mother gave her enough. She had spent her childhood being a mom to her younger brothers and sisters, so she was never nurtured. This was her second childhood. For some reason, she called Melinda "Auntie," which drove some of the women crazy.

"If Miss Brenda's your mama, then Melinda's your sister, not your auntie," Quincey said.

Charmain shook her head. "It doesn't matter how old you get, you come across different people in your lives who take on different roles. When I met Miss Brenda she felt like a mama to me. And Melinda felt like an auntie. That's just how it is. So leave me alone."

Some still went to the bathroom with the door wide open. At dinner time, they'd still fight over their place in the buffet line, even though there was enough food for everyone. They still heaped on as much food as possible. But they weren't eating as fast as they had. And we would have dinner conversations and remain seated until the final person was done. Suzanne, the Queen, was always the last person to finish.

They still needed major etiquette lessons. At least once a week we were invited to a potluck dinner at a church. I tried my best to explain to the women that a potluck didn't mean all you can eat and take home. But every time, without fail, the women would gorge themselves. And then, just before it was time to go, they would get back in line and pile yet another plate to maximum capacity, placing a napkin over the mountain of food before trotting out to the van.

"Don't do that," I would say, cringing. "You're acting like I don't feed you. If you're still hungry, there's plenty of food back at the house."

But it didn't matter. Every time there was a buffet dinner, they would behave as if it were their last supper. They simply thought that if they let you eat as much as you wanted at dinner, you should be able to take it home too.

"It was really good, so we want some for later."

I had to choose my battles. I stopped arguing with them and let them take as much food as they wanted. And every time, Melinda and I would roll our eyes and cringe.

Some evenings after dinner we'd sit in the library and talk about our day. Sometimes the women would tell stories from their past. When they had arrived, they were ashamed of their lives. Over time, they learned how to laugh at the ridiculous things they had done during their life of crime. So much in their past was so sad that I'd sometimes feel sick listening to their stories. The only way to relieve the pain was through laughter. Sometimes I couldn't believe we were able to find humor in their pasts, but we did.

On occasion, the women took special delight in shocking me with their stories; they liked to watch my reaction. After a while, they began to see their actions through my naive eyes. I thought I had led a worldly life, but I had been oblivious to the world they had lived in. They thought it was really funny that I knew so little of the world that was normal to them. I never judged them, and I think because of that they felt safe opening up. Instead of being embarrassed, they'd compete for laughs. We'd howl at some of their stories.

Even Shay, who was closemouthed when it came to her past, had us in stitches one night.

She would conduct what she called a "prostitute survey." She asked the women to tell about the weirdest things a john would ask for. She told us about one of her johns who had a foot fetish: "He picked me up in his car and told me to hurry up and take off my shoes. Well, I was living on the street, hadn't taken a shower in more than a week, and hadn't taken my tennis shoes off in just as long. So I started taking them off, and, wow, my feet stank so bad even I could barely stand it! I cracked the window a bit, trying to hide the smell. But he told me to put my feet up on the dashboard. 'Hurry,' he said. I was so embarrassed 'cause my feet were so dirty and smelly—just plain *nasty.* But I put them on the dashboard for him, hoping he wouldn't notice. Well, he got one look at my sorry feet, shook his head, and said, 'This isn't what I had in mind.' I hopped out of the car as fast as I could, 'cause I'd already gotten paid!"

I know it seems strange that we laughed at stories about hooking and drug dealing. But I believe this helped the women view their lives from a different perspective. They distanced themselves from their past by laughing at the insanity of it. When they could laugh at their past, it no longer defined them.

They were becoming less and less the people they had once been.

We did not have one fight. Sure, we had arguments and disagreements—the women were rough around the edges. But I found that refreshing. What you saw with them was a lack of hypocrisy. They didn't care what most people thought. They'd just throw it out there. After being around so many women who thought one thing and said another, I really enjoyed the honesty.

Shay loved cooking the meals, but to tell you the truth, I didn't like pig intestines and stomachs and God knows what else. Tiffany was always eager to clean; Charmain had a need to clean too. The Queen would just sit there as if we were her servants.

Before bed, we'd hang out in the living room and play board games.

Sometimes we'd watch TV—televangelist Joel Osteen was popular. We watched movies. I loved comedies, especially Tyler Perry movies. We laughed hysterically at Madea, and we did impressions of her famous expression, "Hellerrrr."

After tucking in Charmain, I'd head off to bed. A few minutes later without fail, several of the women would come in to my room to ask me questions before they went to sleep. They were like little children, procrastinating at bedtime. They'd stay in my room, sitting on my bed or on a chair as I tried to sleep. For them it was a big slumber party—the one they never had as girls.

They'd ask me questions about my childhood. They all wanted to know how I grew up to become the person I became. They couldn't believe I had such strong relationships with all of my children. They would ask me about my daddy and mom. I thought about how embarrassed I'd once been when I told people I'd spent my early childhood living in a trailer. Sometimes I had even lied about it. But to the women, my trailer-park childhood made me more like them, and my girlhood stories were like fairy tales.

Sometimes the subject would turn to their lives, and bedtime would become a counseling session. I would sit with one of them, asking the others to leave to give us privacy. I'd try my best to help her talk through her life and sort things out. We would grieve over whatever had happened. Many times we would cry over childhoods that were never to be. The child who should have grown into a woman of destiny was still a child trapped in a woman's body, struggling to figure out her future.

All her growing up would have to be done in a collapsed time frame at Hob Hill.

I also realized one night while sitting on my bed that my destiny was to help the women discover their destinies. Even though we were so different, we were also alike. I had spent years struggling to find my place in the world. Finally I knew where it was.

I felt like Dorothy from my favorite book, *The Wizard of Oz.* Dorothy really didn't know what she was doing or where she was going. But she had these three beings following her around, trusting her to make the right decisions so they could get what they thought they needed. What they didn't realize is that they already had what they needed—they were brave, they had heart, they were smart. Even Dorothy, who had been so lost, so far from home, had it within her to return home. The wizard taught them to use what was already inside them, dormant and waiting to be discovered.

That's our problem—mine, the Loveladies', everyone's. We don't use what we already have. We're all like Dorothy, the Tin Man, the Cowardly Lion, the Scarecrow. We spend lifetimes chasing dreams and searching for happiness when all the time it's right inside each of us. God has a plan, yet we waste time running from it. That plan is the only thing that can bring us peace. I promised myself I would never wander off the path He had for me—not ever again.

Nearly every day I would design a new class for the women. There was so much they needed to know. So much I didn't realize they didn't know. Every day there would be "a new fajita on fire"—another thing I took for granted, another thing they'd never seen or heard about or dealt with before.

All of them were terrible at saving money. If they had two hundred dollars in the morning, they'd have zero by afternoon. They had made twenty-five cents an hour in prison, so now they were making real money for the first time—a few hundred a week—and they thought they were rich. They were planning to go home for Thanksgiving, but none had saved any money for their trips.

Suzanne loved to shop at the department stores. Melissa had expensive tastes—especially in shoes and purses. Her motto was, "Buy the shoes; worry about paying the bills later." Shay was addicted to Walmart. But it was Suga-Suga who could outspend them all—at the dollar store. She'd bring home loads of trinkets for herself and the other women.

"What the heck did you get that for?" I'd ask her when she'd hold up some cheap figurine. She'd look at me with a blank expression. "I dunno. I like it."

"In the library!" I'd yell.

I took a bunch of white envelopes and handed them to the women.

"What are the things you want to buy this week?"

The women rattled off what they wanted: Vaseline, lotion, shoes, cigarettes.

(I hated that they smoked, but I knew it was unrealistic of me to ask them to quit.)

"Okay, label one envelope your 'hygiene' envelope. Label another envelope for clothes. And label another envelope your 'bad habit envelope'—that's the one for cigarettes. You'll all be traveling soon, so remember to have a 'trip' envelope. You'll need money for bus and taxi fare. That's going to be a big part of your expenses. You'd better start saving."

They wrote their names on the envelopes, and we figured how much they had to save in order to buy what they needed and wanted in each envelope category. Tiffany had seen a pair of black high-heeled shoes at Walmart that she couldn't stop talking about. She was already planning what she would wear with them.

"Suga-Suga, you can't afford those shoes right now. Maybe in a month."

"But I love those shoes. I don't want to wait."

I loved Suga-Suga like a daughter. She and I were inseparable. She followed me around the house, studying how I did everything—cook, clean, even answer the phone. The other women were jealous of all the attention I gave her; they called her my pet. Yes, I would have loved to get in the car with Tiffany and buy her those shoes myself. But I knew that wouldn't teach her anything.

"For heaven's sake, stop buying all those trinkets for everyone and start saving your flippin' money."

With my black Sharpie, I wrote SHOES on an envelope. "The minute you have enough money for those shoes, I'll take you to Walmart myself."

For four weeks Tiffany stopped buying trinkets and lotions and whatever else caught her eye. She saved enough money for her beautiful high-heeled shoes, so I drove her to Walmart. She was so excited, but I was nervous. She had her heart set on that pair of high heels. I feared that four weeks later, those shoes were long gone.

When we entered Walmart, Tiffany headed toward the shoe department. I grabbed her arm.

"Suga-Suga, I don't want to disappoint you, but I'm sure those shoes are gone by now. Maybe you can find another pair."

"No. I want those shoes, and I'm going to get them."

She flashed a mischievous grin as she skipped over to the shoe department, taking a detour toward the men's section.

Tiffany might not know how to budget, but she was smarter than everyone thought. She had hidden her beloved high-heeled shoes in a box way in the back of the men's shoe section—and there they were waiting for her. She smiled victoriously as she held the box in the air.

And that's how we handled financing.

I'd hear the women talking about some man they hoped to see when they were home for Thanksgiving.

"In the library!"

I called this class "Looking for Love in All the Wrong Places." I would play that song from *Urban Cowboy* as they settled into their seats, armed with pad and paper. Then I'd ask them about their relationships, where they met their men, what they did together. None of them had ever been in a real loving relationship. They didn't know anything about love or courtship or dating. I was shocked by how they would meet a man in the afternoon and by evening move in with him.

I told them that I'd made mistakes too. My first husband was a violent man who had hit me. I had stayed with him for too long. Actually, I never left. He left me.

"I know you're all heading home hoping to meet up with the men you left behind. But you can't go back to the man you were with when you were committing crimes or using drugs. You can't go back to that kind of man or you'll just get in trouble. You can't be a different person with the same kind of man you used to be with. For now, you shouldn't be with anybody. Relax. The man for you will come to you. And when he does come, you don't move in with him on your first date!"

They didn't like the idea of waiting one bit. I knew Shay had a boyfriend,

Frank, who was bad news. He was a married man, and she was just a prostitute for him, but Shay didn't understand this. He'd buy her gifts, so she thought he loved her. She proudly showed off a silver necklace he'd given her.

"Is he married?" I asked.

She rolled her eyes at me. "Yes, he's married. But we're just friends. I can call him and ask him to pick me up and he will pick me up no matter what. That's a good friend."

I nodded. "And that's it?"

"Of course that's not it," she replied, annoyed by my ignorance. "I would have to do something in return. That's how it works."

Shay said this as if it were the most natural thing in the world, as if that's how it worked for everyone, as if that were normal. And it was normal—for her, and for most of these women.

"Shay, do you really think I am that stupid? That necklace is a yoke around your neck," I said. "He's just paying for it, honey. As long as you're hanging on to him, you're not ever going to be free. He's your sugar daddy. There's no difference between a hooker on the street and what you're doing with Frank. He's a ho too. And he's nowhere near a friend."

As I spoke she rubbed her necklace.

"Take that thing off," I said.

Shay scowled at me, but she unclasped it. I knew when I wasn't around, she'd put it on again. (I found out years later that she did wear it when I wasn't around. One day, it fell off and she never found it. She never saw her "friend" Frank again either.) But that day, Shay wasn't listening to me. In her eyes, Frank loved her and I didn't know what I was talking about.

When Jeff was in town, I'd have him talk to the women about relationships. Some of the women—Melissa, Shay, and Tiffany—who were so used to being abused by men didn't know what to expect from a man like Jeff, who just wanted to help them without asking for any sexual favors. Years later, Shay confessed to me that she was almost insulted at first that Jeff and the other men who visited her at Hob Hill didn't make passes at her. Melissa agreed, saying she kept waiting for Jeff to ask for something from her. It was all they knew.

Jeff, who initially had been opposed to my whole-way house idea, found himself drawn to these injured souls after a few months. They'd ask for his perspective on men, and Jeff would counsel them from a man's point of view. He couldn't believe how they'd come to expect abuse in a relationship the way most of us expect fancy dinners and flowers.

"You are special and you can do better," he'd tell them. They hung on his every word. For many of them, Jeff became a father figure. Soon they called him Pops. Melissa, who had always had problems with men, could listen to him for hours.

"You're a beautiful girl with a great spirit," he told Melissa. "And when you decide to get married again, I have to meet the guy first to make sure he's good enough for you—just like a dad's supposed to do."

"In the library!"

We spent weeks before Thanksgiving preparing for every possible scenario the women would be confronted with.

Many they were visiting over Thanksgiving had hurt them. Shay had volatile relationships with her sister, her children, and other relatives. She had always solved her problems by fighting. Quincey had been to a few anger management classes by now, but they didn't seem to be working. I was worried they'd get in fights and wind up back in prison.

"What are the things you expect to hear when you go home?"

"They'll tell me I'm just like my mother," Tiffany said.

I thought about that. "Well, you just say, 'Yes, my mother and I have had our problems. I may not be perfect, but I'm getting better.'"

"You're nothing but an old crackhead," Shay said.

"Well, you tell them, 'That's in the past. I'm working on myself. And just you wait. It's going to be great.'"

Their biggest fears were being exposed to drugs.

"What about friends or family doing drugs in front of us? Or asking us to do drugs?"

"You just run. Then you scream, *'Get thee behind me, Satan!'*"

The women laughed uproariously. "We can't do that. That's crazy talk."

"Yes you can. You scream as loud as you can."

They looked at me like I'd lost my mind.

"Okay, if that doesn't work," I said, "tell them you're calling the cops. They'll leave you alone then."

"You're crazy. You don't snitch on a friend."

I thought for a moment. "Well, what if there was a rattlesnake coming at your friend? What if your friend was on the sofa not paying attention to the rattlesnake and it was crawling toward her, fixing to bite her on the neck? You'd yell, 'Move! There's a rattlesnake!' And you'd expect her to move. You're either going to let her sit there and get bitten or you're going to say, 'Move, you dumbass!' You'd want to save your friend, right? Well, that's not snitching; that's saving."

As the women packed for their trips home, I packed for Gulf Shores. It would be the first time I had relaxed in a while. Besides working with the women, I was still working with Jeff in real estate. That weekend a house was about to close, and we desperately needed the money from the sale to cover our increasing expenses. Stephanie, my assistant, would take care of it for me. A few years earlier, I had reluctantly hired her, but she had proven to be a hard worker. I was spending most of my time and money on the whole-way house, so I relied on Stephanie to do my job as well as her own.

I knew she and the other employees were annoyed that I wasn't there as much as I used to be. My interest in the business seemed to diminish a little more each day I spent with the women. And now I worried what would happen when they were on their own over Thanksgiving.

What was I thinking letting them go home?

"Mother, they'll be fine," Melinda said. "They love it here, and they don't want to mess up. We've taught them well and they will do great."

I kept reminding myself that I promised not to hold these women captive by too many restraints. But I wasn't ready. I wanted to lock these women in a room in complete restraints.

I was petrified. I worried they'd all relapse.

I worried I'd never see them again.

15

Stephanie

A thief believes everyone steals.

Edgar Watson Howe

If it hadn't been for the Loveladies, I never would have done what I did. I had known Mrs. Brenda way before all the Loveladies came and took over her life. Suddenly she had no time for anyone but Shay, Tiffany, Suzanne, Parthina, Melissa, Quincey, and Charmain. She had forgotten about me.

I first heard about Mrs. Brenda from a teacher at a local college where I was taking some classes. She said if I had a mentor, I could really make something of my life. She told me to look up a local businesswoman named Brenda Spahn and see if she could hire me. I needed a job and was worried about paying all my bills. I was taking care of my two children as well as my drug-addicted husband's three children. I was twenty-six. All my life I had been dirt poor. Maybe this woman could help me fulfill my dreams of success and wealth.

So I walked into Tax Max, Mrs. Brenda's tax-preparation business, and asked to see her. I was told she was too busy to meet with me. I wouldn't leave. I sat my big butt down in the lobby while everyone stared at me. Finally this Mrs. Brenda said she would see me. I marched into her office and asked her to hire me.

She looked me over, tried to stifle a laugh, and said, "No thanks."

I told her what my teacher had said. She said she appreciated the kind words. But I could tell she wanted to strangle my teacher.

"I'm sorry. We have nothing available," she said firmly.

I walked out feeling horrible, but I couldn't blame Mrs. Brenda. I didn't look very professional—I was wearing army fatigues, and my hair was long, straggly, and dyed all these different colors. I was also overweight. Everyone had always told me, "You would be so pretty if you lost weight. You have a beautiful face." But I knew what that really meant: "You're fat. Why don't you quit eating?" I guess fat people can't be pretty. Or get good jobs.

As I was thinking these things, Mrs. Brenda walked up to me.

"Okay. I changed my mind."

I stood in the parking lot, speechless, while she marched back to her office.

I showed up at seven the next day. Mrs. Brenda was already there. She looked me over—I was wearing the same clothes as the day before. She smiled and said, "Do you have any other clothes?"

"I have three outfits, and this is the best of the lot."

Mrs. Brenda didn't look too pleased. As her staff filed in for the day, Mrs. Brenda barked some orders and then told everyone she would be out until lunch.

"We're going shopping," she told me.

She took me to Avenue, a plus-size store for women, and bought me lots of clothes. Then she took me shoe shopping. We went to a salon where my hair was rinsed of all its dyes and cut short. I had my fingernails and toenails manicured.

I felt transformed, like a whole new person.

Mrs. Brenda told me all the things I was saying and doing wrong. She corrected my grammar.

"If I'm so bad, how come you hired me?"

She smiled and corrected me yet again: "If I have so many unprofessional issues, Mrs. Brenda, why are you willing to give me an opportunity to work with you?"

I waited for her to answer her own question. "Because, Stephanie, you have heart and determination. Those traits cannot be bought. Clothes can be purchased, but what you have cannot be." With that, we picked up all our shopping bags and I walked into my new life.

Mrs. Brenda had seen something in me that no one had ever seen, even me. She became a mother to me. I'd grown up with a mother who had mental problems and was in and out of hospitals. My father liked to give me and my two little sisters what he called "good old-fashioned whippings." He'd make us take off all our clothes, have us bend over the bathtub, and beat us until we were black and blue.

Mrs. Brenda was unlike anyone I'd ever known. She was so driven and so successful. She had so much money and spent it on clothes and jewelry and vacations all over the world. But she also had a big heart and gave a lot of her money away.

That's why I didn't think what I did was a big deal.

Mom (that's what I had started calling her) would forgive me.

I worked long, hard hours; absorbed everything like a sponge; changed my speech; and did my best to do a good job, to make Mom proud and glad she hired me. It wasn't easy working for her—she demanded 110 percent. She'd get really angry if anyone did not do their best. There was no hanging around the water cooler in that office. But she'd also throw these great big parties and invite all of us to come.

I started out as a receptionist. Then I worked my way up to personal assistant for Mom and Mr. Jeff. I worked sixty-hour weeks and learned everything about the company. I sold houses. I could do underwriting and credit counseling. There was nothing in that company I couldn't do.

But what she did not know was that life at home was becoming incredibly worse. James, my husband, was abusing more than the drugs—he was beating me. He hated the new me.

I did not want the redneck country life with nothing. I wanted more—I wanted a life like Mom's. He didn't. He wanted pills and beer. And for me to sink into that hole with him and forget about Mom, a career, a life.

I wanted to tell Mom about all my problems, but she was obsessed with rehabilitating ex-convicts. I became angry at her for forgetting about me while she helped those women. Couldn't she see I needed help too? I really needed her, but when I tried to tell her what I was going through with James, she just threw her hands up in the air and said, "I'm done! I'm not going to help you unless you leave him."

How could she abandon me like that?

James said he would change if we got a fresh start and moved to Florida. "I'll stop drinking and doing drugs," he promised. There were more job opportunities for both of us there, he said. He seemed genuine. But how could we? James had spent all our money on Loratab, Oxycontin, and Roxies.

We had no money to start over.

Or did we?

Mrs. Brenda had given me so much responsibility—including access to her checking account. Over Thanksgiving, she'd be out of town with her family, and she would have no idea I'd stolen the money until she returned. That would give me plenty of time to cash the check and start my new life.

It was her fault I was forced to do this. She had forgotten about me.

Besides, she'd eventually understand and forgive me.

And one day when I was rich, I'd pay her back.

16

Thanksgiving

Two kinds of gratitude:
The sudden kind we feel for what we take;
the larger kind we feel for what we give.

EDWIN ARLINGTON ROBINSON

During the four-hour ride to Beau's house in Gulf Shores, I couldn't think about anything but the Loveladies. Had I been crazy to let them loose so soon after their release from prison? They'd been in my makeshift program for only a few weeks; they'd been on the streets and in prison most of their lives. How could our work compete with the siren's call of the underworld?

Would I ever see them again?

Before the women left, I lectured them nonstop. I talked so much I'm sure they couldn't wait to get away from me.

"I know lots of programs you've been through labeled you addicts," I said. "They say once an addict, always an addict. But I don't believe it. You all have the power to change."

I thought I'd use myself as an example: "Let's pretend I weigh 320 pounds."

The women laughed. (I may be overweight, but not that overweight.)

"I am not 320 pounds, thank you. But what if I was? And what if I decide I no longer want to weigh 320 pounds and I use everything within me to change? I eat right; I exercise. Finally I'm 120 pounds. Am I still fat? No. But I may be prone to overeat. If I'm not careful, I could be fat again. But all I have to do is use that inner person God created and do whatever I can to stay focused, to stay thin. It's the same for drugs or sex or whatever else is your weakness. Remember that. You are not addicts. Don't let anyone convince you otherwise."

I studied them. Did they understand? I eyed Parthina, who had smoked crack nearly her entire life. She nodded her head. "Yes, Miss Brenda," she said. "Don't worry about me."

I was worried. I thought about turning the car around a million times and heading back to Hob Hill. I'd call the girls and demand they return to my house. We'd have a quiet Thanksgiving at the house, where I could keep them safe.

No, they could do this. I could do this. I had to relax and trust them. I had to believe in what we had accomplished.

The Loveladies weren't the only ones with Thanksgiving plans. I was spending the long weekend in Gulf Shores with Jeff, Beau, Miranda, and Jeff's son, Jason, and of course my little Hunter. Melinda would spend Thanksgiving with her in-laws in Winter Haven, Florida. Matthew and Rebekah were heading to Rebekah's grandmother's home in the Smoky Mountains. Stephanie, my assistant, who had distanced herself from me over the last few months, would be visiting me at the beach to do some Christmas shopping.

Melinda and I had a plan. We would take turns checking in on the women twice a day—morning and night. I also planned to make surprise calls during the day. Maybe even in the middle of the night.

"And you better be where you're supposed to be," I'd warned them all.

"We will be," they had said in unison.

My heart raced as I dialed them on Thanksgiving. Each woman answered right away, so I was able to relax and enjoy the holiday.

In the South, Thanksgiving is about turkey and dressing, mashed potatoes, cranberry sauce, macaroni and cheese, and green beans. Traditional to our Thanksgiving meals is my homemade red velvet cake and famous strawberry salad—frozen strawberries mixed with crushed pineapple, crushed bananas, pecans, and strawberry Jell-O and topped with sour cream. (I always have to make two because Beau insists that Cool Whip tastes better than sour cream. He's wrong.)

But my favorite Thanksgiving tradition has nothing to do with food. While we're eating, we take turns sharing something we are grateful for that year. When it was my turn, I knew exactly what to say: "I'm thankful to God for showing me my destiny."

I'd never felt more thankful, more fulfilled. The women were changing, but so was I. I'd spent all my previous Thanksgivings being grateful for all my things but knowing there was a deep void inside me. Finally God was making me the person I was meant to be.

Happy Thanksgiving.

On Friday, I called the women again. They picked up right away. I was so pleased by how well they were doing that I congratulated myself with a Brenda tradition—Black Friday shopping.

I have always been a Black Friday maniac. When my children were younger, we would wake up early and go shopping as a family. I found out years later that some of my kids hated my beloved tradition, especially my youngest daughter, Miranda. She said I would dress her up to look like a Christmas tree—stringing blinking lights into her long hair; she felt ridiculous parading through the malls as people gawked at her. That morning, as I had done every Black Friday since I could remember, I raced to the enormous shopping mecca Tanger Outlets. I had a system for my Black Friday shopping. First I'd peruse the newspaper for special sales and coupons. Then I'd start at one end of the outlet mall and work my way to the other end. In between, I'd head back and forth to my car, filling it with packages. By the end of the day, I could barely see out the back of my SUV.

Shopping has always been my hobby, my sport, my therapy. When I shop, I'm on a mission—to get as much as possible. But that year shopping at Tanger Outlets wasn't the same. I got bored with it. It made me feel empty. I thought to myself, *I will never do this again. I'm done.* The old Brenda—the shopaholic, the materialistic woman—was dying.

As much as I loved Gulf Shores, I couldn't wait to return to Hob Hill and my girls. My life was no longer my own, and I loved every minute of it.

Not everyone was happy with the new me.

While I was at the outlet mall, I'd checked in with Stephanie, who was supposed to meet me for lunch and some shopping. She told me she would be there in a few hours, after she finished work.

But she never showed up. Then she stopped answering her phone.

I knew Stephanie had become very resentful of the Loveladies. Whenever I told her I wouldn't be able to spend time with her or go to lunch, she would roll her eyes and say, "I know, I know, the girls." She bristled at the mention of the Loveladies. She was not alone. Other office workers were annoyed with me because my focus had shifted from making lots of money to rehabilitating women. And if I didn't make a lot of money, they didn't either. While they were still doing well, they weren't doing as well as they had when I was driven by money, money, money.

My children—except for Melinda—had also come to resent the women.

"You are not their mama—you're *my* mama," Matthew would say whenever he heard the women calling me Mom, Mommy, or Mama. "I don't want these women calling you that. Make them stop it." Beau was equally infuriated. "What in the world? That's not your mama! That's my mama." He said this to one of the Loveladies as if he were a small boy rather than a grown man.

Miranda, my funky, quirky daughter who always spoke her mind, was afraid of the women and stayed as far away from them as possible. Beau, my big-hearted son, was very kind to them and often had them in stitches with his great sense of humor. But he also confided in me during that weekend: "I'm so sick of those women. I'm sick of you talking about them. They've taken over your life."

On Saturday as I prepared for a walk along the white sandy beach, I checked in with the women yet again.

"I'm good. This is the first time I've been sober over the Thanksgiving holiday. I didn't know I could have fun this way," Tiffany told me. "I love you."

"I love you too, Suga-Suga."

I hung up and silently congratulated myself. If Tiffany could make it, they all could. I'd called nearly all of the women. Each was doing great. The doubts and fears I had earlier had been unfounded. The holiday weekend was coming to a close, and everything had gone smoothly. By opting to give these women freedom, I had taught them an invaluable lesson—they could have fun without getting high. Soon they'd be ready to live normal, productive lives.

Despite all the naysayers, despite all the people who had told me I was a fool for giving them passes this weekend, my program was proving a success.

I dialed Parthina, the final call for the day. As soon as I spoke to her, I'd take my walk and spend some time with Beau, his wife, Kim, and their three little children, Micah, Lizzie, and Noah.

Parthina's phone rang and rang. It went to voice mail.

"This is Brenda. Where the heck are you? Call me immediately."

As soon as I hung up, I called again. No answer.

I dialed Melinda.

"Don't worry, Mom. Parthina is fine. She loves the program and is doing great. She'll call you back. Just give it a few minutes. Calm down."

I couldn't calm down. There was a sick feeling in my stomach that she was not doing great.

"Where the heck is she? This is all we asked her to do, and she's not answering her phone! Where can she be?"

Squeaky-voiced Parthina, the woman who had been so quiet, so reserved, so hard to read, had been the perfect resident. Even from the moment she got out of the van, she had never given us trouble. She always did what she was supposed to do. She came to all my classes. She cleaned her room. She went to church and her appointments. She didn't give me attitude like Quincey. She didn't scare the women like Shay. She didn't have to learn everything from scratch like Tiffany.

She wasn't on a cell phone all day like Suzanne. She didn't brag about her street days like Charmain.

She always had the right answer, no matter what the question was.

Then why did I feel so panicked? Why did my gut tell me something was wrong?

It hit me. Because something *was* wrong. While the other women were loud and flawed and colorful, Parthina had been almost invisible, like she wasn't really there at all. She didn't talk during the classes unless I asked her something. She didn't talk during dinner. Yes, she always gave the right answers. But did she really mean a word of what she was saying? Was she telling me exactly what I wanted to hear? During the last month, had I reached her at all?

Of course I have! Haven't I?

It hit me like a punch to the soul.

No, I haven't.

I called again.

No answer.

I told Beau I was leaving a day early. I believed if I were back at Hob Hill, I'd be able to manage the situation better. Plus, all the other women would be returning soon, so I might as well prepare for their arrival.

"Those women again," he said, staring at me with those deep blue eyes. "It's always those women."

Beau is my oldest child. I had him when I was only twenty—still a child myself. When he was a baby, I had been so poor and so unhappy in my marriage. Beau was the joy of my life, and we were inseparable for six years until his twin siblings, Melinda and Matthew, were born. I love all my children fiercely, but I have always felt a special closeness with Beau because we practically grew up together. Actually, I liked to tell people that Beau raised me. He had been born an old soul. He was a big teddy bear with a boyish face topped by red hair—the same color as mine.

When Beau had moved permanently to Gulf Shores a few years earlier, he had thought Jeff and I would be following. But now he knew that wouldn't be happening anytime soon—and he knew it was on account of *those women.*

He didn't understand the new me. Sometimes I didn't either.

But one day he would.

On the way home, I dialed and redialed Parthina. Still no answer. This wasn't a case of a misplaced phone. She was either avoiding me on purpose, she was too high to care, or…

I didn't want to think about the other scenarios.

I called Melinda.

"Parthina has gotten herself into some hot mess," I said.

She didn't argue with me. Melinda's optimism sometimes bordered on naiveté. It could drive me crazy. Now even she was no longer optimistic. I felt the last drops of hope drain out of me. I could also tell something else was bothering her.

"Have you heard from Stephanie?" she asked.

"No. I have not. And she was supposed to be in Gulf Shores yesterday."

"Oh."

"What is that supposed to mean?"

"Something's going on. She was supposed to deposit a fifty-thousand-dollar check for a closing, but she didn't."

Stephanie was not the disappearing type. Maybe she was home sulking. Maybe her husband had gotten into some kind of trouble. He was another hot mess she should have walked away from a long time ago. But she was convinced she could save him.

"Don't worry. It's probably sitting on her desk in the office."

There was a long pause. "No, Mother, I checked. It's not there."

What?

If Melinda had driven to the office as soon as she returned from her vacation, she must be very worried. And if my eternal optimist is worried, well, then I should be terrified.

I couldn't find Parthina. But I knew exactly where Stephanie would be. Instead of exiting the highway to Hob Hill, I drove to her house.

I knocked on her door. "Stephanie!" I yelled.

No answer.

"Stephanie!"

I walked to the side of the house and peeked into the kitchen window.

My heart jumped into my throat.

The house was stripped bare.

There was no Stephanie. No James. No kids. No furniture. No signs of life. Nothing. Stephanie had moved out without telling me. A woman I had trusted as much as any member of my family had disappeared without a trace.

And she'd taken a check for fifty thousand dollars with her.

Happy flippin' Thanksgiving.

17

The Aftermath

For if you forgive others their trespasses,
your heavenly Father will also forgive you.

MATTHEW 6:14

I was furious. I couldn't remember a time I'd felt this angry, this betrayed. I held the phone in my hand, hoping Stephanie would call and offer a plausible explanation. I also prayed that any minute, Parthina would walk through the door at Hob Hill.

Stephanie wouldn't steal from me. Parthina wouldn't leave the program.

As it got later and later, I realized I was wrong.

The Loveladies had returned from their Thanksgiving pass, but Parthina was not coming back, and Stephanie was long gone.

"I told you so," Jeff said. He had never trusted Stephanie and didn't understand why I kept giving her more responsibilities. I knew many of my employees felt the same way. I had thought I could prove them wrong. I believed that by giving her a mother's love and helping her change, she'd overcome her character flaws. Had I wanted a new life for Stephanie more than she did? Stephanie wanted to change her financial situation—she wanted money and possessions—but maybe she didn't really want to change herself.

I'd spent the last month teaching the Loveladies the importance of forgiveness. As I sat in my chair, nearly paralyzed with anger, I realized I was a complete hypocrite. The Loveladies had been raped and beaten and hurt by so many people, and I had told them to forgive the people who had done these acts to them. But would I forgive Stephanie?

I kept thinking about that money. We desperately needed it. Every month I was spending more money than I had planned. We had so many expenses. I thought about how just a few months ago, that sum wouldn't have meant that much to me. Now, it represented food, clothing, and Christmas presents for the women and their children. Some of them had never been able to give their kids presents, and I wanted to help. We needed that money.

Back at Hob Hill, the women told me stories from their Thanksgiving break, but I didn't hear a word they said. I nodded my head and smiled as if I were listening. I couldn't concentrate on anything but the anger festering inside me. How could Stephanie have done this? Had she been lying to me about everything? I thought back to the day five years ago when she walked into my office—her hair a mess of tangles, dressed in camo. My instinct had been to let her walk out. But I had felt a flicker of sympathy and invited her into my life. Had she been thinking about stealing from me way back then?

And Parthina. I dialed Parthina's parole officer. He seemed accustomed to these calls. It happened all the time. Parthina had violated her parole. Once found, she would nab an escape charge and be back at Tutwiler.

"She would rather be at Tutwiler than here," I said incredulously. "Why would she give all this up?"

"She talked a good game, but I wasn't sure about her," Shay said. "I don't know how she could leave all this and choose that world out there."

I had been really worried about Shay. She had been in prison the longest. She had been on the streets the longest. She'd been on drugs the longest. But she was the first one back. Even though she didn't say it, I could tell she was glad to be back. Even though she was angry and full of hate most of the time, she knew this was her home and she didn't want to jeopardize her life here. Even though we still had a long way to go, I believed Shay would make it.

But I'd been wrong before.

For some reason, only Shay was able to lift me out of my mood. She was such a beautiful, complicated woman. I could feel the goodness shining inside her, even if it was trapped behind a barbed-wire fence.

"She wasn't done getting high," Shay said matter-of-factly.

"Did she tell you this? Why didn't you tell me?"

Shay rolled her eyes. "She didn't have to say nothing. She still had her mind on the streets. I could just tell. The whole time she was here, she was thinking about that crack pipe. That's all she wanted. She don't care about your fancy house and that Posturepedic. She don't want anything out of life but to get high."

"How do you know all this?"

"'Cause that was me for a long time." Shay went on, "When you wanna get high, it's all you care about. You don't care about your family. Your friends. Your kids. You don't care if you live or die. Nothing matters except getting high."

I nodded. I realized how little I still knew about the lives the women had come out of. And now more women were scheduled to come stay with us. I vowed that in the next few weeks, I'd learn everything I could about drugs and addiction. I'd also have to come to terms with the fact that Stephanie was gone and I'd most likely never see that money—the money this program could really use.

"So, Shay, how was your time in Mobile? Did you get in any trouble?"

"No ma'am."

"Did you have a good time?"

"Pretty good. One of my daughters was pretty ugly to me. She yelled and told me I'm nothin' but an old crack whore."

I could see the deep hurt in her brown eyes. Ever since our trip to Walmart, Shay couldn't fool me. She was the most sensitive person I knew. I hated that her daughter couldn't get over the past, but I understood. It was a lot to forgive. More than I've ever had to forgive.

"Oh, good Lord, Shay, what did you do?"

Shay smiled. "I said, 'You must be talking to Casper, 'cause that's not me anymore and it never will be.'"

She headed upstairs to her cozy yellow room with the Peace plaque on the door. I knew she'd turn on all her lights and fall asleep on her Posturepedic.

I smiled.

And for a moment I forgot all about Parthina and Stephanie.

Shay was home.

18

Ghosts of Christmas Past and Present

He who has not Christmas in his heart
will never find it under a tree.

Roy L. Smith

I love decorating for Christmas. And I don't mean get a tree, hang some ornaments, sing some carols, and call it a day. I mean a Brenda-style, weeks-long decorating marathon. I'm talking:

- twelve (count 'em) Christmas trees, each with its own theme (beach, teddy bear, bird, Santa, and so on)
- dozens of wreaths
- a few life-size singing-and-dancing Santa and Mrs. Clauses
- a giant snowman who warbles "Frosty the Snowman"
- stuffed animals dressed in red and green
- enormous red, green, and gold candles
- blinking lights
- mistletoe in at least a dozen places
- glittery garland
- holly, ivy, poinsettias, knickknacks

I'm talking decorating so obsessively that the minute Thanksgiving ends, the rest of my family runs away from me. I could scatter a room in a matter of seconds anytime between Thanksgiving and Christmas with the simple phrase, "Will you help?"

My family drove me crazy with their refusal to assist me in my holiday merriment. But when I was done, they loved to bring their friends over to show them "our" decorations. When they moved out of the house, my children said they were glad they would never have to deal with my ridiculous decorating. How did I—Mrs. Claus—ever raise such Scrooges? (After a few years on their own, both my boys ended up decorating just like me—and now their wives could kill me for it!)

When Jeff and I first married, I casually mentioned right after Thanksgiving that it was time to decorate for Christmas. He didn't think too much about it, and we both headed to the garage to begin pulling the Christmas decorations into the house. Hours later, we were still lugging Christmas storage bins in from the garage. "What is all this stuff, and will we ever be done?" Jeff asked, exasperated. Jeff saw chaos. I saw beauty and Christmas cheer.

After that first Christmas, Jeff left me to do the decorating myself. Sometimes I thought I could scare Jeff into helping: I would climb the fourteen-foot ladder and dangle precariously as I hung garland, lights, and mistletoe. Every time I went up and down the ladder, I'd huff and puff, looking over at Jeff, hoping he'd volunteer to help.

But it didn't work.

Jeff would simply glance at me and go back to watching football on television. From that Christmas forward, I was on my own.

And then the Loveladies arrived.

I was more excited about the holidays than ever before. I felt like a new mom showing my kids Christmas for the first time. By now, the parole board had released twenty women to the house. We quickly converted the garage into a bedroom and bought more beds for each room. Some of the women told me they had never celebrated Christmas. Others said they couldn't remember a sober Christmas. Others had such bad Christmas memories they wouldn't even talk about the holiday. They hated Christmas.

Well, I was going to give them the best Christmas ever! The women would attend parties! They would sing Christmas carols! They would dance in a pageant! They would receive presents! They would wrap presents! They would bake Christmas cookies!

I would make sure they celebrated a lifetime of Christmases this year.

I was so excited to have much-needed help. The women and I lugged bin after bin of decorations into the house. With twenty women helping me, I figured we'd make the place a perfect winter wonderland in just a few days.

First, we assembled the artificial Christmas trees. They were all different sizes—from six to fifteen feet.

"This is going to be beautiful," I said as I fixed the limbs of the trees so they matched my vision. As usual, I already knew exactly what the house would look like when we finished decorating.

The women worked on different trees in different rooms of the house, and I walked back and forth, supervising. I smiled as they oohed and aahed while unpacking ornaments. They held the ornaments gently in their hands and showed them to each other as if they were prized jewels they had discovered during some archeological dig. I closed my eyes and tried to imagine Christmas through their eyes—so new, so sparkly, so thrilling.

And so confusing.

Somehow our visions were not merging. They had no idea what they were doing. As I checked on their trees, I saw that they'd clumped all the lights in one section. Again, I was shocked by how little they knew how to do. They were really children in adult bodies.

"We have to space these out," I explained as I pulled the lights off and demonstrated how it should be done.

But no matter how much I explained, it seemed the women couldn't figure it out. The trees looked horrible. The decorations were bunched together. The garland was a tangled mess. There were bare spots where the lights should be.

"Angels do not go on the fruit tree, honey."

"Darling, the Santa does not go on the angel tree."

"Sweetie, those Christmas balls belong on the tree, not in your ears!"

I struggled to be patient, which has never been my forte. I couldn't stand the job they were doing.

The women smiled at me, proud of their accomplishments. I smiled back.

Then I looked around and immediately wanted to tear my hair out. The house was in shambles. My ornaments were strewn about the floors. The women were singing carols, decorating their hair with *my* ornaments and wrapping my big Christmas bows around their waists.

Shay was dancing with the mechanical life-size Santa who sang "Jingle Bells" over and over. The women thought it was hilarious that Shay was acting so silly. *Do they not understand that Christmas decorating is serious business?* I was trying to make the holiday magical for them, and all they could do was laugh and joke around. They didn't care if it looked good or not.

What a mess!

Then the women started arguing over which trees looked best. Did they really think these disasters looked good? The women in the dining room felt they were the winners. I eyed the dining room tree and thought I might have a heart attack. If this was the best tree, I was afraid to look at the worst. The tree—with its sequined fruit balls, birds, pine cones, and feathers—was a jumble of decorations, some turned the wrong way, some hanging from the same branches. And what was a Santa ornament doing in the middle of it? Did they not see my themes? But the women who claimed that tree was "theirs" thought it was the best ever.

I couldn't take it anymore, so I decided to distract them with a different job.

"Go get the tree skirts," I yelled to Tiffany. I figured I'd have them arrange the skirts around the base of the trees while I fixed the mess. As I waited for Tiffany, I redecorated the dining room tree in my head. I'd have to take off most of the ornaments, restring the lights, redo the garland—basically start from scratch.

Never again.

"Tiffany!"

Tiffany walked into the room with the tree skirt wrapped around her waist.

"I don't understand how this works," she said, her face full of childlike wonder. "I can't get it to fit right."

Oh, my. I couldn't believe it. She thought the tree skirt was an actual skirt!

Then it hit me.

This hadn't been a disaster at all. This had been a success. I had been so wrapped up in my vision of perfection that I almost missed how perfect this moment had been.

These women had never had a real Christmas. Their lives had been devoid of tree skirts and garland and Christmas trees. They had no idea what they were doing. But they were having a wonderful time doing it.

I thought about those past Christmases when I had made so many people miserable with my endless, mindless decorations. I thought about my children, who had tried to decorate with me, but it was never good enough. I wished I had not wasted all that time with things that did not matter. I had worried more about perfection than the imperfect people helping me. How could I have been so selfish?

These women were so giddy, so excited, so flawed yet so perfect.

I started to smile. Then I laughed—so hard my face hurt. I laughed at Tiffany in her tree skirt. The other women laughed with me, but they weren't sure what they were laughing about.

"What did I do wrong?" Tiffany asked, looking upset.

"Nothing, Suga-Suga. That's a great idea," I said.

I picked up a tree skirt and wrapped it around my waist. The other women did the same. Tiffany started dancing to "Jingle Bells," and soon we all joined in. I thought about all the women who were less fortunate than I am, and I danced for them. I thought of all the women who never dance, and I danced for them. I thought of the women who have never celebrated Christmas, and I danced for them.

I started crying.

Tiffany looked at me. "Did we not do it pretty enough, Miss Brenda?"

I looked at the lights, the decorations, the trees, and our tree skirts.

"Suga-Suga, I have never seen such beauty."

19

Tiffany

If you fell down yesterday, stand up today.

H. G. Wells

It was the best Christmas ever. So why did I mess up? I never had a Christmas before. It was just another day to get high. But this year, I did a lot of things I'd never done before. Decorating. Christmas caroling. Going to my first real Christmas party.

The night of that party, I felt like a real princess in wine-colored pants with a flowing jacket to match and my hair all curled. I'd never worn makeup except when I was prostituting, and that makeup had been nothing that Miss Brenda would have approved of. On the night of the party, Miss Brenda and Miranda helped us all with our makeup and we looked so beautiful.

Miss Brenda had invited a lot of people to the party—all her normal friends. So everyone stared at us when we walked into the fancy country club. The other guests stayed far away from us. I felt like we had a big sign on all of us that said Fresh Out of Prison.

Melissa was mouthing off about how those people thought they were better than us. Miss Brenda's friends were at one side of the room. We were at the other. Miss Brenda kept running back and forth to each group. She'd ask us to go over and meet her normal friends, but we wouldn't. We watched as she'd run over to her friends, and we knew she was begging them to meet us. We could see them shake their heads no.

Poor Miss Brenda looked like she just wanted her own party to hurry up and end. She had been so excited about this party, telling us how it was a tradition she had for many years and how fun it was. We knew most of her friends were not excited about us or her new life.

She came back to us all, smiling. "Come and meet my friends," she begged again.

"They do not want to meet us."

"How are you ever going to make it in the free world if you don't meet people who haven't been in prison?" she asked.

After a while, our little group got sick of sitting there like we were under a microscope. We were all dressed up and ready for a party, but acting like we were still stuck in prison. This was the first time I'd been at anything like this. It was the first time I'd been at any party without anything to drink.

"This is big-time. We're at a country club. I've never even seen anything like this except on the TV," Shay said. "And we're all standing around looking like scared little boys. We should be jamming."

"I don't care who those people think we are, I'm dancing," Melissa said.

Shay, Melissa, and Quincey headed to the dance floor, so I did too. The Electric Slide came on and we started dancing. Then some of the regular people got up and danced too. We showed them our moves, which were a lot better than the way they danced. I could move real good too. Then we made some requests to the deejay. So the deejay played "Get Low," a hip-hop song with lots of f-bombs in it.

We were shaking our booties real good by now. I happened to glance up and there was Miss Brenda looking at us with her mouth all open, like she was ready to explode. She ran over and screamed at the deejay, "Turn that off!"

Then she ran over to us.

"What the heck are you doing?" she asked us.

"Dancing."

"Well, you're dancing like you're selling something. Ladies do not dance like that," she hissed.

I thought I moved real good and so did her lady friends because even when we stopped moving that way, they kept on dancing like we taught them. They were having a good time.

Her friends weren't so bad. They were pretty nice.

Then someone brought out a karaoke machine.

Everyone said I should get up and sing because I'm always singing around the house, but I was really scared. Singing around the house is a lot different than singing in front of a bunch of normal people. But they kept at it, and the next thing I knew, I was up on stage, singing "No More Drama" by Mary J. Blige. It's my favorite song. Mary J.'s my favorite singer. I felt like she shared my life—she was abused when she was a little girl. She had sex and used drugs to try to feel better. Her song was like a message to me. She understood me. It's a song that's like a prayer to God, asking for the pain to go away, asking for peace of mind.

Singing is what kept me sane during my addictions. I love to sing. But I was so nervous I almost forgot the words. I thought I did a terrible job. But after I finished, everyone clapped so hard and for so long. I thought, *Wow! I must have been really good.*

We left that party feeling like it had been another magical evening. We forgot who we really were. We were just regular people. Miss Brenda always told us that Jesus is King and we are all His princesses. I laughed at her saying this because Oreo never ever felt anything but ugly. But that night I thought, *Miss Brenda is right. I am a princess.*

Princess Tiffany.

The next day I left for Dothan to visit family. The day after Christmas, I went to the playground to see my playmates. That's what we call it in rehab—playmates and playground. My friend said she had some stuff for me. I said no. I thought of Miss Brenda and thought she would be proud.

We were at a club, and after a few minutes, I decided to go to the bar. I ordered a shot of gin. I felt like I would be okay with that. I could drink but I wouldn't use. Then I ordered another. After a while, I lost count of how many I had.

Then I went to find my playmate.

"Okay. I'm ready to get high now," I told her. We went outside and I took a big hit of crack.

I was so upset when I woke up the next morning. I had gotten high my whole life. This was the first time I ever felt so bad about it. This time had been different. I knew I had people who loved me. I had a family who cared for me, and I'd let them down. During the last few weeks, I had learned there was another way of life than the way I had been living. I never knew that. All I had known was drugs and doing what I had to do to get them. It was all bad. I liked crack because it took me out of that life. I knew I didn't need to escape anymore.

I also knew I was done. December 26, 2004, would be the last time I would ever get high.

But was it too late?

I was so scared to go back home. I was afraid Shay would know the minute she saw my face. I figured I could hide it from Miss Brenda and Melinda and probably the rest of the Loveladies, but not Shay. Shay knew everything.

I walked in the house all casual, and there was Shay by the door. I gave her a big hug and a smile and she never suspected a thing. I had passed the test and fooled her. I felt good. I had nothing to worry about now. If Shay didn't know, Miss Brenda wouldn't either.

I walked toward Miss Brenda, trying to act like happy Suga-Suga. She looked at me hard. "Oh, Tiffany, what did you do to make yourself so unhappy?"

I couldn't speak. I didn't know what to say. When I was on the street, lying was something I could do real good. But Miss Brenda saw through me and I couldn't get any words out. I just started crying.

I cried and cried. I thought I would never stop.

"I'm sorry. I'm sorry," I said.

She was so upset with me. "How could you?" she said over and over. "Don't you know that you're a fool to call those people your friends? They hate you. They want you to go to jail. Those people you hang out with are not your friends and never have been."

"What are you going to do? Please don't tell," I begged. "I'll never do this again."

The other girls crowded around me and begged Miss Brenda too. "Please don't tell on Suga-Suga." I felt so loved, like this was my real family now.

"We can't sweep this under the rug. I have to report this or I could get in big trouble. I have to tell it like it is," she said.

"Can I stay? Please?"

Brenda looked at me like I'd stomped on her heart with those high heels from Walmart. She always had an answer for me, but this time she didn't. I knew it was going to be bad. I would probably be sent back to Tutwiler. That judge had been right—there was no hope for me.

I had been a princess. But it just turned midnight.

Instead of losing a shoe, I was losing my life.

20

Relapses

I didn't fail the test, I just found
a hundred ways to do it wrong.

BENJAMIN FRANKLIN

When Tiffany walked in to Hob Hill, I knew. She tried to hide it. She smiled. She gave me a big hug. But I looked into those hazel eyes and could see her sorrow staring back at me.

One of my most fervent prayers when I started the ministry was to ask God to equip me with the gifts I would need to be able to detect the lies. I knew I would be dealing with women who were much more streetwise than I, and I knew they could certainly out-lie me. I have been granted that gift. Sometimes I feel like a human lie detector.

The minute I saw Tiffany I knew she had used drugs.

I was heartbroken. Tiffany had been like a little girl filled with such joy in her new life that I was shocked she had gone back to her old ways. I know that sounds naive. I didn't yet understand the hypnotic power drugs had over these women. And I know I've said I was heartbroken before—I was still reeling from Stephanie's betrayal and Parthina's departure. But nothing hit me like Tiffany's relapse. I felt knocked out. I had worked harder with Tiffany than with any of the other women. If she couldn't make it, maybe the program was doomed.

The women heard Tiffany's sobs and gathered around us. They knew how much I wanted this program to work. They understood there was a lot of pressure on me from the authorities, who were scrutinizing me. They knew Tiffany had begged me not to tell, and they knew it would have been easy for me not to tell. As Tiffany cried, they pleaded with me to keep it to ourselves. Suga-Suga was everyone's baby girl.

"She'll never do it again. It could be our secret," they begged.

"That's not how we operate," I said, although I dreaded making the call and wished I could make this our little secret.

I was terrified. If Tiffany was sent back to prison, that would be the end of Suga-Suga. She'd never make it. She would fulfill the predictions of all those officials who had labeled her a hopeless case. When I dialed her parole officer, my hands trembled. This felt like the most important call of my life. Would I be able to save Tiffany? Or would she get lost in the system until she died?

All of them, except Tiffany, who couldn't stop crying, were holding their breath as I spoke to Charles, her parole officer. Charles worked with most of the women in the house and had gotten to know them and me. I explained to him that Tiffany had relapsed during her pass.

"I know no one thinks she will make it, but I just think she is this diamond in the very rough. I really believe that my program is the best thing for her and that she has a chance if she stays in it," I said. "Charles, there is something about that girl that I just love."

I held my breath, my heart pounding.

"I love that girl too," Charles said. "Okay, we'll let her stay, but she can't pull this again or she's out."

"Thank you!"

I hung up the phone, closed my eyes, and exhaled. "Suga-Suga's staying," I said. I was elated, but I kept my cool. I punished Tiffany by revoking most of her responsibilities. She was essentially starting over. I prayed that she was really finished with drugs—because she wasn't going to get another chance. But I wasn't sure. With Tiffany, I couldn't be sure of anything.

The women were ecstatic. Suga-Suga had become everyone's favorite. She had become the unofficial social director, singing and humming and helping all the women with their problems. When a new woman arrived, Tiffany would swap bedrooms so she could sleep in the same room as the new girl and have a new friend. She'd give the newbie a tour of the house and fill her in on the different personalities, the different classes, the jobs, the Hob Hill gossip. Suga-Suga was on a quest to have as many friends as possible. She was succeeding. Everyone loved her.

But ever since Tiffany's relapse, Shay wouldn't talk to her. She wouldn't even look at her. She'd serve Tiffany her food with a scowl.

"Why do you have to be so mean?" I asked Shay. "All the women are scared of you. You boss them around. You yell at them. You're just so nasty to them."

The women couldn't stand Shay. A few had played nasty pranks on her. One time, Shay flew down the stairs, screaming, "I'm going to kill her!"

"Who?" we asked, all terrified she was speaking about one of us.

"Annette, that's who! Where is she? I swear, I will kill that girl. She put ants in my bed. They're everywhere! And not just little ants. These ants are four times the size of normal."

I tried to calm Shay down. "You don't know it was her."

"Of course it was her. She's always out in that garden. She's the only one who had the guts to bother with those big ants."

"Shay, it was probably an accident. Did you have food on your bed?"

"No. They were dumped in the bed. Then Annette put the sheets and covers up so I wouldn't know until I was in them."

Annette, who had been in Tutwiler for drug possession, had arrived a few days earlier. She and Shay were always at each other.

I found Annette, who was on gardening duty. I told her to keep her distance from Shay.

"She says you emptied a jar of big ants all over her bed."

"I didn't do it," Annette said, laughing.

"Annette?"

Annette laughed. "I swear to God. But I wish I had thought of it. I can't stand her."

We tried to discover the culprit, but we never did find out who did it—

although Shay remained convinced it was Annette. Another time, one of the women wiped her bottom with one of Shay's prized plush terry cloth towels. (She loved to talk about those towels in her praise report.) We never figured out who did that either—by then, there were too many women who might have.

"Can't you just try to be nice to them?" I pleaded. "Then you won't have to worry about ants in your bed or nasty stuff on your towels."

"I don't want to be around them. I want nothing to do with them and their foolishness."

"We're here together and we have to get along. Tiffany's relapse has nothing to do with you."

Shay looked at me hard. "What you call a relapse, I call a choice. It's the same story. We come to this place and things are going good. We have a relationship with God. We begin to understand addiction. Our families slowly come. Our kids slowly come. We are going to live happily ever after. And then *bam*! We just get up and leave and get high. You don't understand. I've seen it so many times now. It seems like it will happen to me if I don't watch out every minute of the day."

Her face was balled up in fury. The root of Shay's anger was always fear. I knew that, but the other women didn't seem to get it. She was a big chicken about everything. She was scared of the dark. She was scared of the highways. She was scared of driving. She was scared of megastores. She was scared of most people. Most of all, she was terrified of relapsing. Shay treated it like a contagious disease the other women had. Her anger was a repellent, keeping everyone at a distance. No one wanted to get too close to Shay. And Shay didn't want their germs.

"Shay, you have control over this. It is in your power."

She looked past me, as if reliving something terrifying that only she could see.

"We all got a ritual we do when we want to get high, even though we tell ourselves we won't ever get high again," she said, her eyes tearing. "I would start walking around the house looking for any loose change I could find. Then I'd find the most obscene outfit I could wear. You wouldn't believe the things I'd put on. And by the time I'd walk down the street, I'd have a trick and some money and then some crack. It was so easy."

I was learning as much as I could about drug addiction. For some reason, heroin and opiates are the DOC (drug of choice) for white people, while black people prefer crack or cocaine. I don't know exactly why this is, but my black residents who had used almost always preferred stimulants, while the white women preferred opiates. Shay was an exception. She had been introduced to heroin as a young girl and that had been her DOC for years, although she moved on to crack and cocaine.

I asked Narcotics Anonymous to come to the house and speak to the women. Two middle-aged women showed up, but halfway through their talk, I decided NA was a mistake. These women bragged about how messed up they had once been, what fun they had once had, all the sex they had had when they were high. Instead of helping the women, they romanticized their past. (And they were wearing Kiss T-shirts. I hate the band Kiss.) I know that NA has helped people with addiction, but it didn't feel like the right answer for my women.

"I want you to leave my house," I said angrily to the startled women, who thought I was in the program, not running it.

After they left, I spoke to the Loveladies.

"Can you imagine being in such bondage that you have to go to meetings for the rest of your life? That woman said she went to meetings every day or she'd use," I said. "NA says you are powerless over your additions. I say you're not powerless over anything."

Shay nodded her head. "I used to go to those meetings, but by the third one, I'd be using with someone from the meeting."

I invited other counselors and therapists to speak to the women. Although NA asserts that a belief in a higher power will provide the addict with strength to overcome addiction, I felt it overemphasized a person's powerlessness over addiction. I felt it encouraged an addict to rely too heavily on a human sponsor.

I wanted a program for the women that was spiritual but also treated drug and alcohol abuse as a curable rather than a terminal disease. I discovered one that was perfect for them—Celebrate Recovery, a Christ-based approach to recovery founded by pastors John Baker and Rick Warren (author of the bestseller

The Purpose Driven Life). The program treats addiction along with encouraging spiritual growth. It stresses that through prayer and meditation, a person can become free from addiction while developing a stronger relationship with God.

I know many people don't agree with me, but I truly believe that an addict isn't always an addict. I believe that an addict can become free from addiction.

"You only need one sponsor—Jesus," I told the women. "When you look to a person instead of God, you are going to be disappointed. A person can always let you down. That person is one decision from a relapse—just like you. But God is never going to relapse."

Terry had arrived a few weeks earlier. She was a very pretty twenty-three-year-old blonde who came straight from Tutwiler. Ken whispered to me that they had to stop on the way and buy her some clothes because the prison hadn't given her an outfit—she still had on her state whites.

I hugged Terry when she came to the house, but she kept her arms at her sides. She immediately asked for a phone so she could call her mother. She called and called, but there was no answer. Every free moment, Terry would trot over to the phone and try again.

We all tried to love on her. Even Shay was drawn to this injured soul. I think she saw a bit of herself in Terry. I think Shay also felt a maternal instinct that had eluded her when she was a drug addict.

Shay sat on the couch with Terry for hours. She'd hold Terry while the girl cried about her past—I knew she'd been horribly abused as a child. I cried too as I watched Shay reveal such a caring, nurturing side to a person she barely knew. Shay was my Tin Woman—she had no idea what a huge heart she had.

"Baby, it's going to be okay. We're your family too and we love you," I heard Shay tell Terry.

Shay would also make special meals for Terry. She loved showing off her southern cooking, especially to the newly released prisoners who had subsisted on prison slop. That was Shay's answer to all the girls' problems: "Let's feed them." Shay was so proud of her cooking. Everyone gained so much weight when they arrived that we began to call it "the Lovelady spread."

Terry couldn't remember the last time she'd celebrated a birthday, so when her birthday rolled around, Shay decided to make a party of it. She baked Terry a strawberry cake with strawberry icing. We sang "Happy Birthday" while Terry wore a tiara. For the first time since she arrived, Terry seemed happy.

Shay beamed too. "It does my heart good," Shay told me, her eyes glistening. "All the things I missed with my daughter, I'm getting now with Terry. I feel like I'm loving on my oldest girl."

But all Terry wanted was her real mother. Whenever she spoke about her mother, she glowed, as if lost in some distant memory of her. It seemed like she loved her mother almost to the point of worship. Days went by and her mother did not call her back. I phoned Ken and asked if he could find out why Terry's mother wasn't returning the calls.

Ken called back. "She says she's too busy."

Terry would sit with me while I was putting on my makeup in the morning. That was our alone time. In the evening, she'd come into my bedroom and stay long after the other women left. She'd talk about her mother as she gave me manicures and cried.

"I just want her to love me," she'd say. "Do you think she loves me? Why isn't she calling me back?"

I didn't know what to say.

Finally Terry got through to her mom. They talked, and Terry begged her to visit. A date was set up.

The morning of her mom's visit, Terry was so excited. She spent all morning doing her hair and makeup and picking the perfect clothes out of the donations we'd received.

When her mom arrived, we were all curious about this woman whom Terry loved so much. Her mom breezed into the house in a dizzying blur, barely seeing Terry as she came in. "You've gained a lot of weight," she said. Then she told

Terry she didn't like her hair color. She didn't like her outfit or her makeup either. She never bothered even to say hello.

"She's nothing but trouble," she told me as if Terry weren't standing next to her.

By now I had grown accustomed to the frustrations of family members. Usually I could handle an awkward situation and could help connect family members. Not this time. I tried to talk to her, but nothing I said seemed to make any difference. There was no motherly love in this woman.

Terry begged her mother to take her to their house for a short visit. Finally, the mother relented and off they went.

As I waved at the doorway, I prayed for things to go smoothly, but I had a suspicion they wouldn't.

Within an hour, her mother's car screeched to a halt in the driveway and Terry flew into the house, crying. Her clothes were torn, her makeup smeared, and her hair a complete mess. Her mother followed, nearly hysterical.

"She's crazy," she screamed. She said that while they were driving down the road, Terry had suddenly opened her door and jumped out of the car. Terry tried to give her version but was sobbing so hard I couldn't understand her. I told her mother to leave, that I would handle it.

When her mom left, I tried to speak with Terry, but she just clammed up.

After that, Terry slid into a deep depression. Nothing we did seemed to help her—not even Shay's cooking. She kept to herself and seemed lost and unreachable.

"She's not done using," Shay told me. "She talks about the pills she used to take and how they made her feel." Shay shook her head. "I don't understand that pill thing at all. I don't see spending money on a pill and then waiting a half hour to have your prescription filled. When I used, I wanted an instant high. I wouldn't want to wait. Just shoot me up. But she sounds like she would do anything for one of those pills. She's not near done."

A few days later, Terry came downstairs for breakfast. Her eyes looked wild.

Her pupils were tiny pinholes. I had heard from another girl that she had used, but I had hoped it wasn't true.

"Good Lord. What did you do, Terry?"

"What are you talking about, Miss Brenda?"

I laughed angrily. "You're on something right now."

Terry looked at me with such sincerity and such innocence. Drug users make excellent liars. They lie about everything. You could be looking out the window at a beautiful sunny day and they'll tell you it's raining.

"Miss Brenda, I didn't take anything. I would not do that."

"You're lying to me. Don't you know I always figure it out? Stop. It's better if you tell me the truth now, because I will find out."

Terry was adamant that she was clean. "I would never do that to you, Miss Brenda."

Bringing drugs into the house was a major offense. This not only jeopardized the other women, many of whom were overcoming their own addictions and could easily relapse, but this could jeopardize my whole program.

Terry sobbed. "I can't believe you would think I'd do that."

I looked at her hard. "Okay. Then you won't mind if we test your urine."

Terry and Melinda disappeared upstairs. When they returned, Terry was more upset than ever. Of course the results were positive.

"Please don't send me back."

"You're a fool," I yelled. "You know the rules. You cannot do drugs in this house. You cannot bring drugs here."

"I didn't," she said, sobbing. "I wouldn't do that to you. I love you, Miss Brenda."

There was only one thing I could do.

Terry's body convulsed with sobs as two parole officers handcuffed and shackled her. I could barely watch. "Please don't let them take me," she choked out, her tear-stained face turning purple. "I promise I will never do this again. Please, please, please. I don't want to go back there. Don't let them take me."

I tried not to cry. Even though I was furious with her, every fiber in my body wanted Terry to stay. I wanted to beg the officers to uncuff her, to unshackle her, to give her a do-over. I couldn't bear to think of her going back to horrible Tutwiler, where she would become another statistic, a prison number, a hopeless case. What would become of her? Would she get another chance? Was this it? Could I have done something different?

Shay had been right. Terry had not been done.

I found out later that Terry had forged a prescription for the painkiller Loratab. Then she walked down the hill, flagged a car, and hitched a ride to CVS. She walked home and popped some pills. Nobody had known she'd left the house.

Prescription painkillers were my new worry as more women arrived at Hob Hill. I was discovering that those painkillers that doctors and dentists prescribe after injuries are dangerously addictive and are potential gateways to heroin. Hydrocodone and oxycodone, known better by the brand names Vicodin and Oxycontin, are opiates that release the hormone dopamine. Dopamine produces feelings of pleasure and provides the foundation for drug addiction. Instead of helping the women kick these vices while serving their prison sentences, the prisons keep them drugged up for their stay. The inmates call it the Thorazine Shuffle. Poor Terry. I wished I could have done better.

I shook my head as Terry's eyes locked with mine.

"I love you, Terry, but there's nothing I can do about this."

No one made a sound. The women watched, their mouths hanging open, as Terry was escorted out of the house, screaming and crying.

That was the moment when my Loveladies realized I was not some crazy red-haired lady playing house with them. I was the real deal. I may make jokes and laugh a lot, but I took my role as the head of the Lovelady house very seriously. If they messed up, I would still love them, but I couldn't keep them. I would turn them in.

After Terry left, no one spoke for the rest of the day.

No one spoke that night either.

21

Shay

Do not say, "I'll pay you back for this wrong!"
Wait for the LORD, and he will deliver you.

PROVERBS 20:22

Miss Brenda called it the F word. She taught a class about it. She said you have to forgive yourself for all the horrible things you've done to others, and you have to forgive others for the horrible things they did to you. She said I was ugly to the other women because I had so much anger simmering inside me. I had to get rid of that anger by forgiving those people who really hurt me.

Miss Brenda made forgiveness sound so easy, but that's because she doesn't live in my body. If she had my life, did she think she could forgive those people? That's just crazy talk. I wanted to change what was in my heart, but I didn't know if I could ever forgive.

Then one day I told Miss Brenda everything so she could see how hard it would be for me to forgive. I guess I finally understood that no matter what I told her, she wasn't going anywhere. So I opened up that closet and let all the dirty clothes tumble out of it. After I finished talking, we both cried. Then she told me to move closer to her on the couch. I usually tried to sit as far away from her as possible.

This time, I sat on her lap.

I'd seen her daughter Miranda sit on her lap all the time. Some of the other women had done it too. They made it look so easy. Nothing was ever easy for me. But I was a little jealous of the other women because when they sat on her lap, they seemed so happy. They became little girls. I'd never really been a little girl, so I figured why not me?

I sat there and Miss Brenda held me like a child. She wrapped her arms around me and our faces touched. It was the most comforting, secure feeling. I wanted her to be like a mother to me. I wanted her to help me live because I didn't know how to. I thought, *This woman really has got my back.* Maybe now that she knew all this ugliness and she hadn't left, I could trust her like you should be able to trust your mother.

We celebrated New Year's Eve by burning our past. Miss Brenda told us to write about all the bad things that had happened to us, all our pain. Then she collected the papers and placed them in a fire pit in the backyard. We stood outside and watched the papers light up the sky in a big bonfire.

"It's gone. I don't want you thinking about it anymore," she said.

I had written for the longest time. I could still be writing.

I was born in Chicago on a super cold morning in very poor conditions. My mother was from Mississippi, and my dad was from Chicago. They were married and so poor. My brother, Ronnie, was born less than a year later. My mom had pregnancy problems and was very sick and had a hard time caring for me, so I was left alone in my crib. I have always wondered if maybe that is why I have craved love all my life. One day my daddy abused my mom. So she got on a bus and carried her two babies to Mobile, Alabama, where her daddy lived. We never saw my daddy again. My mother never would tell me about him. I carry his name but that is all I know. That has always been a dark hole in my soul. I just wanted to know a little something about him. When I was very young, I used to dream that he came and picked me up and took me away with him.

My memories really begin when I turned five and was living in Mobile with my mother and Ronnie. That's when my mother's brother, Benny, came home from the army. He was so big and so handsome in his uniform. Everyone called him "pretty boy blue" because he was so black he was almost blue. He told my mother that he would watch me while he was on leave so she could work at the restaurant and honky-tonk across the street.

My best friend, Carolyn, was always over at the house, and we would giggle and talk about Benny. A few days after he started watching us, he asked us if we wanted to play boyfriend and girlfriend with him. We were thrilled. I can still remember how excited we were to go places and pretend we were his girlfriends. He'd buy us presents and take us out around town for ice cream and treats. We felt so grown up.

Pretty soon Benny explained that the title of girlfriend carried certain responsibilities. If we wanted to be his girlfriends and receive presents, we'd have to perform our girlfriend duties. We wanted the presents, so we said yes, even though we had no idea what he was talking about.

He had me go into my mother's bedroom first. He'd kiss me on the mouth like I was a grown woman. Then he'd touch me and have sex with me. After he was done with me, I'd leave and Carolyn would go in. I was always first. He gave us cigarettes and taught us how to smoke. He told us that all of this was our secret—the smoking, the things he'd do in the bedroom. If we wanted to be boyfriend and girlfriend, we couldn't tell anyone.

Carolyn and I knew the things we were doing were not right. It hurt and we wanted to cry, but we felt we were part of some secret society. Benny kept having sex with us, and we knew we were very different from the other girls our age. I didn't like feeling the way I did. I was so confused, so angry. I wanted to tell somebody, but I didn't. My mother was always busy and working, and she loved her brother. Carolyn and I didn't talk about it with each other either.

Then my mother got married and gave birth to my sister, Tonya. I became filled with hatred for this baby and my mother. If my mother could not take care of me and left me with her brother, why would she have another child?

When I was about ten, I was already developed like a grown woman. I started running away from home all the time, and my mother never knew why. "Why do you have so much hate inside you?" she would ask me. During the day, I'd hang out with my friends. At night, they'd go home and I was a child of the street. My mother would find me and drag me home.

One time my mother, who had found the Lord, decided I needed an exorcism. She took me to a holiness church down the street. The elder put me in the middle of everyone and threw holy water and anointing oil at me. I was so angry. There was my mama looking to her God in church, while her brother was having sex with her little girl in her bed. I hated Benny with my whole being. I hated God too. How could God let a little girl suffer so?

My mother also took me to a psychiatrist, who told her something had to have happened to me that made me so angry and so old for my years. I thought, *Finally someone knows, and I'll be free of all that weight.* I thought my mother would figure it out. Instead, she said, "Nothing could have happened to her." I wanted to yell the truth. The words were screaming in my soul, but they would not rise up to my mouth. I hated my mother for not knowing. I ran away again and again.

In the summer, my mother sent me to Mississippi to visit my grandmother and my relatives, who lived in shacks next to each other on a dirt road surrounded by big fields. During the day I would pick cotton, cucumbers, and purple hull peas until my fingers bled. At night, the adult men would have me come into their beds. The men would not let me near their children during the day, but at night they all wanted to be with me. I was a bad girl, they would whisper to me over and over while they raped me. I heard I was a bad girl so much that it never occurred to me that it might not be my fault. But I learned if I did what they said, I would get candy and cheap little presents.

When I was eleven, I noticed these two beautiful women who were always on the street. At least they seemed beautiful to me. I would hide and watch them. Their names were Ruby Red and Johnnie Mae. They always had money, clothes, and wigs. They always seemed happy. Even though they were on the street a lot, I could tell they had a place to live because they were clean.

One day Ruby Red came up to me. "Little girl, why are you always following me?" I told her I wanted to be just like her. She seemed so proud to hear this. She said there were men who would pay lots of money to have sex with a young girl like me. I was shocked—I would get paid for all I had done for free.

Ruby Red and Johnnie Mae bought me clothes, shoes that fit, wigs, and makeup. They taught me how to shoplift and turn tricks fast. Their motto was, "Find them, service them, and get out as fast as possible." Time was money.

I quickly learned that I had someone else to answer to—Jinx, the handsome, well-dressed man I'd see them with. I learned that the girls had recruited me for him. Jinx made me feel really important because I would hold his drugs for him. He had men line up for me and this time they treated me nice. Jinx made sure of that.

Every day Jinx would give Ruby Red and Johnnie Mae their medicine to make them feel good. One day I asked for it. I was feeling poorly and didn't want to go out, so Jinx relented. Ruby Red stabbed my arm with a needle. I was just twelve.

It was like a burst of light. All of a sudden the abuse, my life, my guilt, my memories, my torment fell away. How could I have known that a simple shot would finish off what the sex had started? No longer did I regret my life. I thought I had made it. No more did I want to be normal—I was better than normal.

That medicine was heroin.

My happiness was short-lived. My mother found me and dragged me home. She threw me in the bathtub and prayed over me. "Satan is not taking my daughter from me," she screamed. I fought her and tried to climb out a window. My mother collapsed into a pile of tears. She called the authorities, who carted me off to my first official home for girls.

By the time I was sixteen, I had lived in five homes for girls. I ran away from every one. Escape was easy. Sixteen was a turning point for me. I got caught with drugs. Lots of drugs. Because of all my escapes, they cut me no slack. I was sent to Tutwiler for six years. I was actually proud because everyone was surprised to see a sixteen-year-old in a women's prison.

I felt like a big deal.

When I got out, I went to Wisconsin with one thing on my mind: Uncle Benny. He had moved there. I went to his house and was shocked by his beautiful home, car, and furnishings. He treated me like an uncle, and it confused me. I thought maybe he had changed. But that night he tried to touch me while I slept on his sofa. I rose up and told him I was not a child and to leave me alone.

I wanted to kill him.

A few days later while Benny was out, I called a friend. He came to Benny's and we loaded everything from Benny's home into my friend's truck. Then we sold his entire house of things. I did not even leave him a shirt. I took his life as he had taken mine.

I decided to use Milwaukee as my home base. I had a place there and would turn tricks. One night, a trick told me he didn't have the money but he'd pay me in three days. I got so angry I couldn't see. In the corner of my room I had a sawed-off shotgun. I beat him in the knees with it and took whatever money he had. He left naked, crawled to a pay phone, and called the police. I was arrested for armed robbery. I served four years in prison—three in Tutwiler, where I earned my GED.

When I got out, I wanted to start a new life. I fell in love with Nose. He was a pool hustler and a pimp, and I was his only woman. I became pregnant with his child. Nose sent me to my mother's when I was five months along. I had my baby, Jamie, and we went back to Nose. I had a dream that we were a family, so I took the beatings Nose gave me. I'd get high and go off and prostitute. One day he beat me up so bad I ran away. No more abuse for me. I left Jamie with my mother.

Some people never learn. I met a guy named Buck and made a best friend named Jenny. I loved her like a sister. One night she met a gambler who was very drunk. She didn't feel like turning a trick, so she rolled him when he got his clothes off. We thought it was hysterical that she got all his money. But this guy found our dealer and fixed Jenny's heroin with battery acid. She died as soon as she shot up. It was a terrible death and scarred me so bad I never shot heroin again. I changed to crack. I never contemplated not using. I just switched drugs. Then I met a new man, and he and I traveled all over the country. I was living the good life—a crooked gambler and a happy hooker. I had determined that staying on the move could keep me out of jail.

Of course there were so many nights and weeks in and out of jails that there is no way to tell about them. There are so many times I nearly died. I had given up on life and really wanted to die. I could tell you horror stories of the men I serviced. I could probably make your hair stand on end with all my close calls.

I became pregnant again. After I gave birth to Charlisha, I dropped her off at my mother's and left. I couldn't watch her and never bothered to go and visit. I didn't care about my daughters. I didn't care about anything.

I just wanted to die. I thought I could sell drugs to get out of the game and be okay. I wouldn't use anymore. I'd do drugs without letting the drugs do me. And I was doing pretty good for a while until a drug dealer set me up with some boys who robbed me. I did what I felt was right. I put a gun to my "friend's" head and pulled the trigger. The gun did not go off. I was out of my mind shaking the gun around, telling him how lucky he was that I didn't kill him. The gun fired. The bullet hit him in the stomach.

I received twenty years for attempted murder.

Off to Tutwiler. I was ready. I was tired and relieved. I was glad to get twenty years and go to prison because I didn't know what else to do. I wanted to die.

While I was in prison, Benny died. I finally told my mother all about what he had done to me. I told her in a very ugly way. I told her she was a failure and did not protect her baby girl. She cried so hard. I thought I'd feel better, but I didn't. I looked in the mirror and I hated what I saw. My inside was so ugly. I couldn't see nothing on the outside that I liked. I hated everything about me.

It was nearly time for me to be released when the warden called me into her office. My mother had died. I had treated her so poorly, but I had loved her so much. I had even imagined that when I was finally released, she would help me become a good person. I didn't want this life anymore. Now she was gone and my hated sister was raising my children.

When I finally was released, I wanted to change so bad. But I didn't know how to live right and do right. I was sent to that crazy do-gooder's mansion. She and her daughter with those beautiful blue eyes that were filled with love told me I was beautiful and a child of God. I was His princess. They treated me like a daughter.

When I'd been there for a few months, Miss Brenda asked me to be baptized.

"Nuh-uh. I've already been sprinkled and dunked to get all the demons out of me. It was horrible and all I did was cry."

"This will be different," she told me. "This will be wonderful."

Miss Brenda explained that baptism is a symbol of washing away the old person. After you're baptized you feel new and clean and good, she said. I wanted to feel that way, but I was so scared. What if I messed up?

When I was on the streets, I used to pray to God. I would say, "Lord, please help me." Then I'd wait for that bolt of lightning. When it didn't come, I'd think God wasn't listening to me, that I was too ugly even for God. I hated God because He didn't care about me. I hated Him because He was a man and all men ever did was hurt me.

Miss Brenda taught me that God is my Father, the King of all kings. There is no bolt of lightning for anyone. I was in a fight for my life.

One weekend, Miss Brenda took all of us to her house in Gulf Shores. I'd never seen the beach before. The sand was white like snow, and the water was this turquoise blue, as blue as Melinda's eyes. It was the most beautiful place. I was always amazed at all the responsibility Miss Brenda gave me. She asked me to drive some of the women around to see the sights there. So we shopped at factory outlets and souvenir shops. I told Miss Brenda that she couldn't send me into those name-brand shops because I had no idea how to act in those types of places. She just looked at me like, "Come on, Shay." She said those people were no better than me.

I bought one of those umbrella hats because I didn't want to get too much sun. We went to the beach and I could have stared at the water forever. We stayed there all day and night, just staring. I kept calling it the ocean, but Miss Brenda told me it was the bay. Same thing to me.

One day, we all went into the shallow water, where we formed a circle and sang. Miss Brenda asked if anyone wanted to be baptized. She looked at me. I nodded. I'd said no so many times, but I was finally ready.

We walked out into the water and I kept thinking, *How much farther is she going to go?* I was so scared of the water and I can't swim. I didn't have a bathing suit, so I wore a pair of shorts and a really long T-shirt that went down to my knees. Finally Miss Brenda stopped. A big wave nearly knocked me down and I grabbed Miss Brenda around the neck and screamed a little. When I calmed down, I looked at her.

"I'm ready," I said.

She gave me the most compassionate look, like a mom really proud of her daughter. It made me feel so loved. Then she put her hand over my mouth and dunked me. She gave me a real good dunking. I didn't want to be held under for more than a hot second, but she held me under for about five seconds and it felt like an eternity.

She was right. When I came up, I felt clean and new and good. I thought,

I am having a different life from now on. Maybe there wasn't a lightning bolt, but if you look at my life at Miss Brenda's compared to my life just a little while back at Tutwiler, it's as if God has taken a magic wand and changed everything. I have real friends. I have jobs and responsibilities. I have a relationship with God that I never thought I would have. People love me. Miss Brenda loves and trusts me as if I am someone real special to her.

Something in my heart is different.

The old me is really, really gone.

22

Driving Ahead

I like the dreams of the future
better than the history of the past.

THOMAS JEFFERSON

Remember how Shay laughed in my face when I told her I'd help get her driver's license? Later Shay came to me and said she really *did* want a driver's license. She knew how to drive, but she had never had a license. She saved her money. She got the driver's manual. She studied. She knew every answer. She could parallel park better than anyone (certainly much better than I ever could).

The day of her driver's test arrived. She left the house nervous and excited but returned a few hours later, simply devastated. She was told that in Alabama, a person with a drug felony has to pay a $275 reinstatement fee to get a new license—even though Shay had never had a license to begin with. This was another example of the system providing extra obstacles to those people who are already struggling to overcome obstacles.

I wrote *driver's license* on one of our budgeting envelopes, and Shay started saving. After a few more months, Shay finally paid the money, passed her test, and received her license. It was one of her proudest moments. Besides her inmate ID card, she'd never had any identification card. Now I had to tell her to put the darn driver's license in her purse and quit showing it to everyone.

One day she didn't feel well, so I sent her to my doctor. A few hours later, the doctor called. I thought something was wrong. The doctor said, "She's fine. But do you know why she kept showing me her driver's license?"

A few days later, I told her to look outside. In the driveway was a navy-blue '92 Buick LeSabre. It wasn't in the best condition—the paint was fading and peeling in spots.

"What do you think of that car?" I asked her.

"Wow! That's a beautiful car."

"Do you like it?"

"Of course I like it."

"Well, it's yours."

Shay screamed. She hugged me so tight. She was a teenage girl with her first set of wheels. I couldn't stop smiling.

"I figured it's about time you got your own car since you're running so many errands here."

"It's for me? It's really for me? Are you sure? Me?"

I laughed. "Who else would it be for?"

We called Shay "First Avenue" because she'd usually navigate the city on just that one road. "You can get anywhere from First Avenue," she'd say. The truth was, she was petrified of the highways.

"Just get on the interstate," the women would beg her so they could get to their appointments on time.

"No. I'm comfortable with First Avenue, and I'm the one driving."

Sometimes, if Shay had a passenger and they were in a rush, she'd reluctantly drive on the interstate. But she would keep her head perfectly still and only stare straight ahead. She was too scared to take her eyes off what was directly in front of her. The passenger would have to look at the rear and side mirrors to tell her if it was safe to change lanes or exit the highway.

The more responsibility I gave Shay, the more she thrived. Part of this job, I realized, was to spot potential in people that they didn't see in themselves. I knew Shay had so much talent. She just needed a chance to thrive.

By now there were forty women living at the house. New arrivals thought Shay was part of the staff rather than an ex-con. I'd eavesdrop as they'd tell her their problems while she cooked. She'd listen and give them advice. Sometimes I'd hear her imitate Melinda or me. Other times, she'd be herself.

"Hang on, sweetie," she'd say. "You can make it. I'm living proof."

The first Loveladies resented the new arrivals. "She's my mommy, not your mommy," Charmain would tell the new women, who would look at her like she was crazy.

The women were all working. Some had jobs around the house—cleaning, gardening, laundering. Some of the women worked at my office—answering phones, organizing, or cleaning. I called friends and asked them to hire some of them, but they made excuses. Most people were afraid of hiring "Brenda's women." So I'd invent businesses. I turned my office parking lot into a car wash. A few of the women would wash and detail cars.

Melissa also drove the women to their jobs outside the house and to appointments, but she was always getting lost. I'd never known anyone with such a horrible sense of direction. She was constantly calling me on her cell phone (I had given in and gotten the women phones) to help her figure out how to get home or to someone's job or appointment. The women were so frustrated with her.

"She's a scatterbrain," Shay would say. "She may be black, but she's got some blond roots in that head."

Once, Melissa got lost and never showed up to pick up Quincey from her job at the mortgage company. Quincey stormed into the house hours after she was supposed to be picked up. I was on the phone when Quincey started screaming about it to me. I put my finger up. *Hold on a minute, Quincey.*

"You don't dare put your finger up at me," Quincey bellowed. "I don't care if you're on the phone. You talk to me now!"

I slammed the phone down and stared. "Quincey, more anger management classes for you."

"No! I finished my classes. I've taken them six times now. I'm done."

"Obviously you're not," I said as I walked away, leaving Quincey cursing and fuming.

I trusted Shay so much that I began letting her run the place while I stayed with Jeff at our home about twenty minutes away or when I headed to Gulf Shores for the weekend. One cold and rainy night, the phone rang just as I had fallen asleep.

"What is it, Shay?" I knew it was Shay before she uttered a word.

"The alarm won't set," she said, her voice in a panic. Then she read me the code that had appeared on the box.

"Oh, that's no big deal. It means the basement door must have opened. Just run down to the basement and shut the door. It probably blew open in the storm."

"You want me to do *what*?"

"Close the flippin' door. I'm tired. I want to go back to sleep."

I heard the other women in the background ask what I had said.

"She said for one of y'all to run on down to the basement and lock the door while I stand by the alarm supervising. Hurry up," Shay said.

I laughed so hard. "I did not say that. I put you in charge. You go down there, Miss Shay!"

My big ex-con was a big ol' chicken. I found out later that she had gone into the kitchen and passed out knives to each woman. While she stayed upstairs "supervising," the women held hands and formed a daisy chain until the first woman reached the basement door and shut it. They were all so afraid of everything. They still slept with all the lights on—except for Tiffany, who was fine with the dark.

Shay was proud of her ingenuity. But the next day I gave her an hour-long lecture. I told her she was their leader. She had to be the one in charge. She had to be the brave one.

"I'm just a big ol' chicken, and I don't think I'll ever change," Shay said. "Even when I was high on drugs, I wouldn't go in the woods to do 'em. I had to have streetlights."

I loved Shay unconditionally. Despite her horrible past, she was one of the most wonderful human beings I had ever known. And she could make me laugh even when she was speaking about her past.

I was so proud of her, so in awe of her. She was a true survivor. I'd look at her and the other women and think, *How can they take so much abuse but still continue?* The human body is such a contradiction. It is so strong and can handle so much, yet it is so fragile and can break so easily.

Shay was still angry deep down; she was still mean. I could feel a shift, though. She'd smile more. She'd laugh more. She didn't yell all the time. When Terry had been at the house, I saw a Shay emerge that I didn't know existed. She was sympathetic and nurturing. She would hold Terry as if she were the daughter she never raised. I imagined that one day she'd not just be cooking, but running this program with me. I didn't dare tell her that—she'd probably have a heart attack. Just like the Tin Man, Scarecrow, and the Cowardly Lion, she had the power within her. She just didn't know it yet.

I was discovering a lot about myself too. I was learning how to help each woman overcome her obstacles. Annette, who was forty and had three children, had been living at the house for a few weeks. I had been struggling to figure her out. I remembered her from the Birmingham work release program. She had attended many of my services and came to my viewing of *The Passion of the Christ*. Annette had just been released from Tutwiler for drug possession. But that wasn't it. She had been in more than fifteen rehabilitation programs and transitional homes, as well as multiple jails and prisons.

When she arrived, I heard Annette and her boyfriend fighting in the driveway.

"That woman is nothing but a cult," her boyfriend yelled.

"This may be my only chance, and I'm going to give it a shot. But don't worry, Jimmy. I will never become one of those Bible-thumping Jesus freaks."

Bible-thumping Jesus freaks? I wanted to run outside and tell Annette to leave. The last thing I needed was someone upsetting my Loveladies.

Annette walked in and told me that she had been raised in a strict Catholic household. "I'm done with faith," she told me. I explained that my classes were Christian-based and that part of the program involved going to church. I held my breath, willing her to leave. "Why," I asked, "did you watch *The Passion of the Christ* with me if you're done with faith?"

Annette grinned. "I love popcorn…and I like you."

"Why did you come to all my services then?"

She grinned harder. "When you're in prison, you'll do anything to break free from your boredom, even if it means going to church!"

She annoyed me. I thought I had been packing the room because of my brilliant preaching, and here she was telling me that it was just an escape from monotony. "Well, are you sure you want to be here?"

Annette shrugged her shoulders. "I'll stay and listen, but don't expect me to change."

I looked into Annette's past. It surprised me. She wasn't a typical Lovelady at all. She came from a wealthy family. And since her father had been in foreign affairs, Annette had lived all over the world. She had been born in Barcelona and could speak Spanish fluently. She had grown up in mansions and had cooks, butlers, and chauffeurs at her disposal. She had two brothers and two sisters who were all very successful. As a child, she dreamed of being an actress and always had leads in the school plays. She told me that whenever she watched the Academy Awards, she became filled with sadness because of the dream she abandoned when drugs took center stage.

What had happened?

I thought I'd heard all the possible stories, but this didn't make any sense to me. Annette had gone to the best schools, had loving parents, lived in a stable home, and was provided every opportunity. I began questioning her, trying to uncover the dark family secret. I kept waiting for a punch line about some family abuse, some horror.

She confessed she never felt like she belonged in her family. As a child she had broken into her father's office looking for adoption papers. She believed she had to be adopted because she was so different from the rest of her family. She never found any papers, and her parents assured her that she was their biological daughter. But she was always on the run and always an outsider. "Why can't you be more like your brothers and sisters?" was her parents' lament.

One day she started using drugs and couldn't stop.

Shay knew Annette from Tutwiler and couldn't stand her. "I was an old-timer and she was a carefree spirit. She'd be in the shower, and she'd throw her dirty clothes right on top of my clean clothes. I can't stand such foolishness," Shay said.

Annette didn't like Shay either. They argued all the time. (Shay was still convinced Annette had put those giant ants in her bed.) Annette was in charge of the grounds and the swimming pool. However, she was all over the place. She would plant a flower somewhere and then run to clean the pool. Then back to the flowers. Then to the pool. She was thin and bursting with energy. She was never on time; she never finished a job; she was never consistent. When the women would sleep, she'd be awake.

Shay would boss her around, bark orders at her, and then tell on her when she didn't complete a chore.

"I hate Shay," Annette would scream.

Around this time, my Hunter was having trouble in kindergarten. He couldn't focus on his schoolwork and had difficulty concentrating. I took him to the doctor. Hunter was eventually diagnosed with Attention Deficit Hyperactive

Disorder—ADHD. As I watched Hunter bounce from one thing to another, it occurred to me that he acted just like Annette.

I called Annette into my office and asked her questions about her childhood, her grades, her ability to concentrate. I finally took her to a doctor. "She has one of the worst cases of ADHD I have ever seen," he said.

Although I am usually opposed to drugs, I begged Annette's parole officer to allow her to take medication for her problem. "No," he said. I did more research. I knew medication for ADHD was controversial, but I also knew Annette was miserable in her own body. She was like a cat chasing her own tail—she'd never be able to catch it. "I feel like I will die using drugs," she confessed.

I told her parole office that I believed Annette had been self-medicating to silence her ADHD. Perhaps if a doctor prescribed a medication to combat her problem, she would no longer rely on other drugs.

Finally, Annette was given permission to take Ritalin. Within a short time, she was a different person. She could carry on a conversation, work in an orderly manner, and sit still for more than three minutes. She was able to plant flowers and clean the pool. Even Shay liked the new Annette. Annette didn't become a "Jesus freak" overnight, but she did listen to me when I taught the Bible, and she slowly developed a strong faith in Jesus.

In time, she reunited with her family and finally felt like she belonged.

Annette taught me an important lesson: sometimes someone's past is not the problem. Many times it is something within ourselves. We need someone on the outside to help us find the answers.

We were like a big family, but the house never seemed crowded. We had developed so many routines at Hob Hill. We'd have classes whenever a group of women had free time.

I spent a lot of time talking about relationships. I believed nearly all of them had no idea how to be in a real loving relationship with men. I'd hear them talking about the guys they'd see during weekend passes, and I'd feel sick.

"You don't take a suitcase on a first date," I'd say. I was always shocked at how sex was just expected in the relationships they'd grown up in.

I'd ask them questions anytime they found a new love: *What's his last name? Where is he from? Is he a Christian?*

They'd respond that they hadn't gotten that deep in the relationship yet.

"Are you kidding me?"

I'd call Jeff into the room to help. Jeff was the first decent man they had ever been around, so they'd pepper him with relationship questions. He told them that a man worthy of them wouldn't expect sex from them. He'd explain that a man should want to get to know them, become friends first, start a relationship. Hearing it from me—the Holy Roller—was one thing. But when they heard it from a man, it had more impact. They loved Jeff, and I knew he loved them too. He'd give them his signature big bear hug and kiss them on the forehead as if they were all his little children.

These days Jeff was around more often. He was spending less time at the beach and at work and more time at the house. It wasn't something either of us had expected. It just happened. I never said anything, although I prayed about it all the time. I knew Jeff could be an integral part of the whole-way house. When we're in sync, Jeff and I balance each other really well—while I am impatient, Jeff is the most patient person I have ever known (he puts up with me). While I get riled up easily, Jeff is always calm and cool. The women needed him. I needed him too.

Every two weeks we'd have a "burn our past" party by the pool. Some women wrote a few sentences; others wrote novels. No one ever read their papers out loud, but we would have a bonfire in the fire pit. We'd all set the past on fire. There would be screaming and hollering as we watched our past become curlicues of smoke, fading into the sky.

"Let's forget about it. It's done. It can't bother us anymore."

The women weren't the only ones who burned their past—I too had plenty of guilt and shame that I needed to burn into ash.

The Loveladies were gaining quite a reputation as spoiled brats among women in other transitional programs, many of whom were jealous of them. Our women showed up at work or program meetings or even parole appointments dressed in the designer fashions they'd found in my closet or in big cardboard boxes or bags that my friends would donate.

Melissa, who loved high fashion, would riffle through overstuffed donation bags as soon as they arrived and always managed to put together professional outfits that made her look as if she were running a Fortune 500 company. She loved her black-and-white tweed pantsuit and would wear it everywhere, even around the house.

One day while they were rummaging through my closet, one of the women pulled out my mink coat. Someone took out a camera and each of the women posed in it. I cringed as they each tried it on and pranced around in it.

You see, I hated that coat—I was so embarrassed by what it represented. It was so not me. Yet I had once proudly paraded around in that coat as if I was the biggest deal in town. Who was that person? I barely knew her now.

It's funny how we change. I had strived so hard to become someone who could talk to people I deemed important. I defined successful people as those who made a lot of money and had a lot of things. Maybe it's because I was raised with so little.

As I heard more of the women's stories, I became overcome with guilt. I had spent years being embarrassed about my past when I'd mention to people that I had lived in a mobile home and that my daddy was a plumber. Now I proudly told everyone that my daddy was a plumber and I was kind of one too. "We both deal with people's crap," I would say. "Just a different kind."

The Loveladies believed I had given up so much to give them a new life, but they had given me a new life too. I had to part with my riches to find riches of the soul. At one time, self-gratification had been my purpose. I was on an endless quest for happiness, which I thought I could buy at a store. I learned that despite what we've been told by the media, by teachers, even by our parents, life's real quest has nothing to do with happiness and everything to do with meaning. There are times I am not happy, but there is never a time when I feel adrift. Now I wake up ready to go and tackle each day with purpose and a vengeance. And that's what we need—a purpose greater than ourselves.

I'd sit in the living room with my motley crew of ex-cons and think, *A year ago, I was on a cruise in the Caribbean or on a jet to Italy.* I didn't have any regrets. I didn't want to be on an exotic island or touring a European city. Being with these women was exactly where I needed to be.

My change was gradual. I didn't notice much of it at first. When I started working with the women, I stopped wearing my mink and my expensive jewelry and clothing because I didn't want to be "that rich lady helping prisoners." Then I realized that making money had been *my* drug—just like crack or heroin or Oxycontin or men. If I wanted the women to give up their addictions, I had to give up mine.

Now expensive jewelry and clothing seemed foreign to the person I had become. I liked how I felt stripped of gold and silver and diamonds. To me, it felt normal and better. The person with the jewelry and the mink wasn't who I really was—it was a costume I had worn to be someone else, someone I thought I wanted to be.

Now I didn't want to wear anything that would set me apart from the Loveladies.

One time when we were shopping at Walmart, a cashier asked me if I was a Lovelady. So I smiled and told her yes.

"I hope you appreciate that woman who runs the place. She's taking real good care of all of you," she said.

I nodded my head and stifled a laugh. "Yeah, she's doing a wonderful job."

My old friends didn't care for the new me. They believed I was judging them no matter how many times I told them I wasn't. They'd say things to me like, "I'm not doing anything worthwhile like you." And I'd say, "God calls us all differently."

Though now I'm following God's plan for me, I wasted so many years being selfish. If I didn't sleep for the rest of my life, I couldn't make up for my selfish years, all that time I wasn't doing what I was supposed to do. I ignored God's calling. I had to face the possibility of prison time and have a house blow away to really hear God's voice.

So when the women pulled out that mink coat, it was like they pulled out a relic from someone else's life. Someone I didn't really like.

Who exactly had I been? The women always wanted to know.

I had listened to their stories. It was time to tell them mine.

23

The First Lovelady

Every saint has a past
and every sinner has a future.

OSCAR WILDE

When my mother was twenty-nine, she was told she would never be able to have a baby. Nine months later, I was born. While most of the Loveladies were unwanted babies, I was overwanted, a miracle baby, a gift from God, the greatest thing to ever happen to my parents.

My father, James Kenneth Lovelady, was a plumber who had a gregarious personality and wanted to change the world. My mother, Catherine, was an accountant who was reserved and cautious.

Daddy followed construction work all over the South, so we lived in a tiny trailer that we pulled behind our car. I was a daddy's girl, and my father took me wherever he went. My mother taught me so much in that trailer. I became an avid reader even before I started school. It was just the three of us, spending all our time together in our tiny home on wheels as we traveled from town to town, sometimes staying in one place for just a few days.

When I was about to start first grade, we settled our trailer in a trailer park in Birmingham. I had never really been around children before and was excited for a more settled life.

The first day of school as I was getting a drink of water from the fountain, a boy called me Butterball.

Butterball?

With that, the spell my sweet daddy had put on me was broken. I went home, looked in the mirror, and no longer saw a beautiful princess with rare-colored hair and fair skin. Instead I saw a fat kid with orange curly hair and a face covered with about two billion freckles. I raced to my daddy and told him what the boy had said. My daddy assured me that the boy was blind and not very smart. But I knew my daddy was the blind one. I decided to let daddy be blind—I liked him that way. But to this day, if I am feeling bad about myself, I look in the mirror and see Ms. Butterball.

Finally we moved to a house in Birmingham when I was about to enter fourth grade. I was thrilled to live in a home without wheels. As soon as we settled in, I quickly went out and met every neighbor in every direction for blocks and blocks. In school, I became an overachiever and a straight-A student. The kids no longer called me names. By the time I graduated from junior high, I won so many awards it was embarrassing—friendliest, most likely to succeed, most popular.

It was around that time when I began the work that would later become my calling. If there was a child who came from a broken home or who was a latchkey kid, I'd take the child home with me. "Can we keep her?" I'd ask my mother, as if I were speaking about a stray dog or cat. My mother would smile and tell me that she could stay for dinner, but she couldn't move in with us because she did, in fact, have a home. I never saw it that way though. I thought we could give those kids a better home, more love, nicer clothes. I wanted to fix everyone's life.

When I was about eleven, Green Acres Baptist Church started a bus ministry in an effort to build its congregation. For three Sundays a bus rattled around our streets as we played, but none of us got on it. No one in our neighborhood went to that church or any other church. But I'd watch that empty bus and feel so sorry for the bus driver. The next weekend, I convinced the kids to ride the bus with me. I'd never been on a bus before and was excited for the adventure.

I had never been to church or Sunday school either, but I loved it immediately. I loved the services, the prayer, the songs, the rituals. After that, I never missed a Sunday morning, Sunday evening, or Wednesday youth session.

One Sunday evening as I stood out in the yard of the church and looked up to the heavens, I had an epiphany: I realized that the same God who created the stars created me, Butterball, with my orange hair, billion freckles, big imagination, and mischievous personality. I stood there, tears streaming down my face. I could feel God's presence in my life. I knew God loved me.

Many years later, many mistakes later, that one night remained a turning point in my life. I knew without a doubt that God was real and He was for me. That night when I got home, I told my mother and daddy about my experience. They said they had gone to church when they were younger too. But that was not good enough for their little evangelist, who immediately began preaching to them about Jesus. I really don't know if they simply gave up that night because they were tired or if they truly gave their lives to Jesus then.

But they soon became bona fide Christians, and we went to church as a family. I preached to them, and when I got older and strayed, they preached to me. Funny how those things can happen.

When no one was in the church, I would practice preaching to an empty congregation. When I felt I'd honed my skills, I started asking my friends to listen to me. They didn't want to, so I bribed them. I did their homework and their chores. I even let them wear my clothes. It was my dream to become a minister whose words could move people and change lives. I wasn't deterred by the fact that there are no women ministers in the Baptist church.

By the time I was a senior, I had slimmed down and my hair had darkened to auburn. My dad found work in Nebraska, and I was left with my young married cousins, who let me do as I pleased. I started partying almost every night. I drank for the first time. My grades dropped, but for a while I still managed to get to church. Rather than rush to sit in the front, I would always be late and sit in the back row.

And then I stopped going.

My daddy and mom decided to move me to Nebraska to live with them. I fell madly in love with a wonderful guy. I hated when it was time to move back to Birmingham. Our long-distance romance unraveled very quickly. I was heartbroken.

For me, falling in love was kind of like riding a bike. I fell off and cried. But I got back on and start riding without letting the tears dry first. I guess I was so afraid of being alone that I didn't allow myself time to heal. I married Cecil after dating him for only six weeks. We were married on a Saturday night in front of a justice of the peace. I wore a green dress. For a while I didn't tell my parents.

I don't think my mother ever fully forgave me for this. I didn't understand her anger, but years later after having daughters, I realized how hurt she must have been. There was always an unspoken pain between us.

I never ever wore a green dress in front of her.

A few months into our marriage, I discovered that my new husband had an explosive temper and could be abusive. We were so young and he had so much anger inside of him. The first time he lost his temper, I was shocked. Almost as quickly as he lost his temper, he would calm down and be the most wonderful person. It was amazing. He had a great personality and could be so charming. I loved him so much.

He convinced me that his anger was my fault. Years later I realized that he was displaying the classic behaviors of an abuser, and I was displaying classic abused-wife behavior. There was no divorce in my family, so I couldn't imagine leaving him. I became emotionally dependent on him. No matter what he did, I made excuses for him.

Beau was born when I was twenty. He had red hair and sparkling blue eyes and a wonderful sense of humor. I adored him but was so miserable that I buried myself in food. I was five foot ten and weighed three hundred pounds. The vivacious Brenda was dead. The little girl who had fallen in love with God had vanished.

I knew I had to divorce Cecil to reclaim my life. Instead, I became pregnant.

I actually believed that another baby might help our marriage. Why do abused women think like that? I gave birth to my twins, Melinda and Matthew.

I had two newborns and a six-year-old. We were so poor. One time I had to put some items back on the shelf because I didn't have enough money to pay for my groceries. I kept only the essentials—plus a box of Fig Newtons, Beau's favorite cookies. When I unpacked the bags, the Fig Newtons had vanished. I cried so hard while I rummaged through the car and the house, searching for the cookies. I was devastated that I'd lost them.

As I rooted around the house, I realized Beau wasn't in the room where I had left him. So I stopped my Fig Newton search and looked for my son.

I found him in the laundry closet—eating the Fig Newtons.

I took a deep breath, dried my eyes, stopped everything I was doing, and sat in the closet with my baby boy. I held and kissed him while he ate his delicious cookies. I prayed that I would figure a way out of this misery. I would be rich and successful. I'd give my children the best of everything.

I promised myself I would never again cry over lost Fig Newtons.

I started a small tax business and janitorial service. I worked day and night. I never did find the courage to leave my husband, but after thirteen years of marriage, he left me.

And I got back on the bike. I looked for a man very different from my first husband, and I found him. Michael was tall, blond, and movie-star handsome. I was married to him for thirteen years and never heard him raise his voice. No one could ask for a better husband—he was just never home. He was a captain in the merchant marine. We had a daughter, Miranda, who is a combination of both of our personalities. She has her father's dry wit and my bubbly personality.

Most of the time, Michael was traveling in Africa. He couldn't come home because we had so many bills to pay and not enough money. We wound up filing for bankruptcy. I thought we could start over financially and as a couple. But Michael stayed in Africa, and we filed for divorce.

Years later, when I married Jeff, he said I acted like I had been single my entire life. He said I really did not know how to be married. I have thought so much about this comment, and there is a lot of truth to it. When I was married to Cecil, I was afraid of saying or doing too much because I did not want to upset him. When I was married to Michael, he was always gone. Out of necessity, I had to be a "single-minded" parent.

After Michael, I stayed off the bike and became devoted to raising my four children and making money. I never wanted to have debts like before, and I was determined to be rich. As my children grew, so did my tax business. What started out as a home office eventually grew to eighteen offices throughout Birmingham.

In 1998, I married Jeff, a successful real estate investor. We lived the American Dream. I had everything I wanted—the mink coat, the big house, the beachfront properties, the fancy cars, the exotic vacations. I worked day and night so I could have even more.

Despite my success, I didn't feel the fulfillment I had expected. So I spent time searching for answers. I didn't know what I was after, but I felt something was missing from my life.

I was a good seeker but, as I've said, not a good listener. I didn't have the patience it takes to truly hear. Often the answer is being whispered right in our ears, but our lives are so loud we can't hear it.

Why do the things of the world scream out at us—money, possessions, stuff that doesn't matter? I listened to those worldly screams. I convinced myself that making money was my destiny. I decided I'd be a good Christian too; I'd go to church and give some of my money to the poor. I could have it both ways: I could satisfy my desire for things, but I'd have enough to be generous with my surplus.

I didn't realize that what seems good enough isn't always good enough. I didn't realize that God didn't want—and certainly didn't need—my money.

He wanted *me.*

The Bible tells us that we have to become like a little child. That's what I needed to do—to reconnect with the God I had fallen in love with when I was a little girl with red pigtails staring up at the sky.

It took a lot for God to get my attention. It took a lot of yelling for Him to get me to listen. He had to bring a group of ex-cons into my house to get me to truly understand the power of redemption—not only for them but also for that little girl.

Today I look into the faces of the Loveladies, and I thank God for where I am.

24

The Crazy Lady and Her Convicts

God moves in a mysterious way,
His wonders to perform.

William Cowper

"God will take care of us." I kept telling Jeff this as I worked fewer hours at our business, while at the same time more of our income was covering Lovelady expenses. Jeff was still selling real estate in Gulf Shores; the mortgage business in Birmingham was chugging along. But he was worried about all the money we were hemorrhaging to fund my ministry. We had so many expenses. My time and money were stretched to the max, and Jeff was not happy about it—to say the very least.

This was not the life Jeff had envisioned when we fell in love. We were supposed to be retiring at Gulf Shores, not spending our retirement on a bunch of ex-cons.

So when the *Birmingham News* called in June about writing a small article on the whole-way house, I thought, *Perfect timing.* Once the community learned of this program, we'd receive some much-needed donations.

See, God is *taking care of us.*

Jeff wasn't so sure. When we're in sync, our relationship is quite balanced. I'm the optimist. Jeff's more pessimistic, always yanking off my rose-colored glasses.

Denise, the *Birmingham News* reporter, visited the house one night while we were having prayer group. She took a lot of notes and called the next day to say she wanted to return. A photographer also came and snapped pictures of us. The women couldn't wait to see the story in print. Denise said it would be somewhere in the middle of the paper's religion section.

I was in Gulf Shores spending the weekend with Jeff when Melinda called, excited.

"We're the lead story on the front page of the *Birmingham News*! But it's not just on the front page! It's on the second and fifth page too! There's a picture of you and one of the girls holding hands and praying."

The headline read, "From Prison to Mansion: Ex-Prisoners Get a Fresh Start."

The article was beautiful. It told the story of the program, the story of Shay believing she'd be my maid, the story of some of the women and the progress they had made.

Why did I feel sick?

I called Melinda back. "I'm heading back to Birmingham."

"Why?"

"I don't know why, but I don't think this is a good thing."

I waited for the eternal optimist to tell me I was being crazy. Instead she said, "Me neither."

"Let's not panic," I said.

The reporter called me on Tuesday to say she had been bombarded by phone calls.

"Your neighbors sounded really upset. They want these women out of their neighborhood. I will be doing some follow-up articles on this."

I hung up and called Melinda.

"Okay, now I think we should panic."

I don't really have neighbors—at least not in the way most people traditionally define a neighbor. There is no one living next to Hob Hill. It's on ten acres of property. You have to drive down a long, winding road before you arrive at a street where neighbors live.

Tom and Carol own the only other house on my street. It is also on ten acres of property. We don't see them and they don't see us. Our driveways spill out onto the same windy road that leads to the main street, where the other neighbors live. The only time I ever happen to see either one of them is on that rare occasion when we both are on the road at the same time. Because the road is so narrow, one of us has to pull to the side to allow the other person to continue up to their driveway or down to the main road.

Tom had been one of the callers to the newspaper, and he was irate.

But he wasn't alone. I started getting hang-up calls. We would get flipped off and honked at when we were driving in our big white van with Loveladies written across the side. No one thought we were a girl rock band anymore. To them, the Loveladies were a bunch of criminals ready to escape.

I couldn't blame them. They thought the way I had on that October morning when a group of convicts descended on my home. *Could that have been only eight months ago?* It seemed like another life.

We were on the front page of the newspaper for days and were a top story on the television morning and evening news. I discovered a petition was being passed around the neighborhood to have the women removed from the house. It cited that I was breaking a zoning law that states no more than three unrelated people are allowed to live in a residential home in Birmingham.

Neighbors started making outrageous claims. They said I had offered to have the Loveladies do gardening for the elderly residents in the neighborhood so we could burglarize them. They said I was running a brothel. They said I was operating a meth lab.

I felt I'd made so much progress with the women, convincing them during the last few months that they were normal and could have normal lives in the community. But with this, the women started feeling just as bad about themselves as they had that first day when they had arrived from Tutwiler. They witnessed the deep hatred the neighbors had toward them and the lengths the neighbors would take to make sure they were not walking around in their backyards.

The library, the room where we developed classes and found common ground, became a refuge for tears and frustration. I worried some might relapse.

One night, as a distraction, I took Shay and some of the other women on a shopping excursion to Sam's Club. I don't know if he followed us there, but suddenly Tom, the irate neighbor, was in an aisle next to us.

"There's that crazy lady and her bunch of convicts," he said loudly. Everyone turned toward us. He pointed his finger at us. "You're a bunch of hookers, convicts, and whores."

The women gasped. I could hear Shay softly crying.

"Hush up, Shay," I whispered. "Keep your head up. We can't be seen crying or they win."

"That's the lady who's ruining our neighborhood," someone else yelled.

"That's it," Shay said angrily. "We gotta do something."

I took a deep breath and sucked in my rage. "We're taking the high road," I said, although I wanted to race outside and slit Tom's tires.

To avoid the heckling, I stopped shopping in areas around my house. Instead, I'd drive a few miles away, where I figured people wouldn't recognize me. I quickly discovered *everyone* knew who I was. After all, my face had been plastered in the newspaper and on television. But instead of being greeted with rage, strangers would hug me.

"What you're doing is wonderful," they'd say. "We love you. Keep up the good work. Don't let a few horrible people stop you."

They loved me if they didn't live near me. They hated me if they did. I was a saint. I was the devil. (For the record, I am somewhere in between.)

Of course, I enjoyed being loved, so I kept shopping in other towns. I was a hero, which was much better than being a pimp, a meth lab operator, or the head of a sinister gardening crime ring.

A few days later, a letter arrived from the City of Birmingham. Inside was a warrant for my arrest. I was charged with operating a business in a residential area. As I drove to city hall, I was furious with the city, with my neighbors, and with God. I talked to Him the whole way there: *This is ridiculous. I've done what You wanted me to do. It's been real, but I am so out of here. If this doesn't stop, I'm moving to Gulf Shores and forgetting about all of this nonsense.*

At city hall, a woman fingerprinted me. "I hate doing this to you," she said, fighting back tears. "This is so unfair."

"It's okay. It's okay," I said. "Don't worry at all. We'll be fine. I'm going to ask for a zoning change, and it'll all work out."

The woman wiped her tears, patted my hand, and looked at me sympathetically. "Oh, honey, they'll never change the zoning."

I swatted the air as if this was ridiculous. "Why wouldn't they? Of course they will. I'm far away from everyone. They'll pass it. I'll hold a neighborhood association meeting and they'll all see how good this really is."

"Well, good luck," she said, sighing.

A few nights later, as I sat reading in my chair in the living room, I heard a strange popping noise. I am deaf in my left ear, so I couldn't decipher the sound and didn't think too much about it. I looked around, figured it was something outside, and continued reading.

The next day when a repairman came to fix our cable, he said, "Did you know a bullet went through your window?"

"What?"

He pointed to a tiny hole in the window that had been blocked by the television. Then we looked at the television cabinet. There was a hole in the back. I opened the cabinet. One of Hunter's Disney cartoon videocassettes tumbled to the floor. I picked it up and examined it. A bullet was lodged inside. The bullet had traveled through the cabinet, into the plastic cover of the cassette, and through the cassette. It was wedged like a tumor between the cassette and the outer plastic cover.

"Oh, my Lord."

"You're going to get us killed," Jeff said. He was furious with the neighbors. He was also furious with me for getting us into this mess.

You're going to get us killed.

Jeff had uttered those same words to me months ago when I had approached him with my whole-way house plan. He thought it was the women I should fear. Now it seemed like the women and I had to fear everyone else.

Had someone tried to kill me? Or was someone trying to scare me?

I was terrified.

25

The Meeting

They hate because they fear, and they fear because they feel that the deepest feelings of their lives are being assaulted and outraged.

Richard Wright

I couldn't believe the crowd. I knew a lot of people would come to the neighborhood association meeting, but I hadn't imagined *this* many. The room was crammed with hundreds of people, many of whom had to stand against the wall in the back. I swallowed hard, preparing to give the most important speech of my life.

The Loveladies were scared, but I had assuaged their fears with my optimism. "Once the neighbors meet you, they'll fall in love with you, just like I did, just like Jeff did, just like my family did," I said. "Just like everyone who meets you does."

"Do you really think this is going to work?" they asked.

The women were terrified that my plan would fail and they'd have nowhere else to go. Would the parole board send them back to Tutwiler? Would they be homeless?

"No matter what, I'm not leaving my mama," Charmain had told me one night as I tucked her in. "You will never get me to leave you. A daughter has to stay with her mommy."

"This was too good to be true," Tiffany sighed. "They're taking our home from us. Where will we go? What will we do? I don't want to go back to prison."

"Don't worry. God's on the throne and He's got us," I said. I really believed it. How could my plan not work? Helping these women was my destiny.

The women raided my closet and the donation bins as they prepared for our meeting. They spent hours trying on outfits, fighting over blow-dryers, doing one another's makeup. I retreated from the chaos of the room to get dressed. When I returned, it was quiet.

"You look so beautiful," I heard one of the women say to another.

"No I don't. I look fat."

"No. You look awesome."

"You clean up really good."

"So do you."

"The neighbors aren't going to believe their eyes."

I walked into the room. The women all looked so beautiful. Even Shay and Annette were dressed up and smiling at one another.

"You look beautiful," Annette told Shay.

This will work, I thought.

"You're each going to walk into the meeting alone and mingle with the neighbors before it starts. Do not talk to each other. Do not sit with each other. Sit next to people you don't know and chat with them. No matter what anyone says to you—no matter how nasty or vile—do not get angry."

I turned to Quincey. "Did you hear that, Quincey? Do not get angry!"

She smiled at me. "Yes ma'am!"

"Okay, y'all tell them you think it's a good thing to help these women. Be respectful when you talk, but talk. I want the neighbors to think you are just concerned citizens, not the Loveladies. They'll see that you are no different than they are."

"But we are different," someone said.

"Yes, you are. You are more special."

"Miss Brenda, are we really worth all of this?"

"These people are no better than you are. They're human, just like you. You made some mistakes. Do you think no one else made mistakes in their lives?

Maybe they did too, but they didn't get caught. You made mistakes, but you're still God's children. And the neighbors are going to fall in love with you."

I told them I would give a speech to the association. When I finished, I'd ask the Loveladies to stand up. The neighbors would expect to see a bunch of crazy-looking, wild-eyed, dirty misfits. Instead, forty-three well-coiffed women would stand. The neighbors would be shocked at how normal my women looked. We'd all just love one another, hug, and laugh about the last few weeks.

"Of course the women can stay," would be the consensus.

Before we left for the meeting, we prayed. I felt confident I was doing what God wanted. I was positive this latest obstacle would have a happy ending. My lawyer, John Amari, a former state senator, seemed convinced we would prevail. And he'd been to enough of these types of meetings to know.

As I stood in front of the audience, I eyed the crowd. The Loveladies were scattered throughout the room, just as I had instructed. Some of them were deep in conversation with the person sitting next to them. I smiled and relaxed a bit. My neighbors would learn that they feared something that was not to be feared.

This is going to work. This will be a wonderful night.

"There's that lying b****," someone screamed at me. "She's ruining our neighborhood."

"A complete loony," another muttered.

Tom was in the back of the room wearing his signature sunglasses. Jeff was standing near him, edging closer and looking furious. I noticed a bunch of policemen scattered throughout the room. "Those women are stealing all our lawn furniture," another person yelled.

I cleared my throat and spoke as calmly as possible. "No one is stealing your lawn furniture," I said. "Why would we do that? We have our own and we don't need more."

Then I began my speech. I explained that I was looking for a temporary zoning change that would have no lasting effect on the property. If we moved, the zoning would reverse back to strictly residential.

"This is just an opportunity to help some women get back on their feet and return to society." I told them how the parole board sends ex-cons back to their old neighborhoods instead of providing them with a second chance. I told them how the women had lived with me for the last nearly nine months and no one had seen or heard from them until the newspaper article.

I thought I had done an excellent job.

"We don't want pimps, hookers, and whores in our neighborhood!" someone called out.

People burst into applause.

"Let them go somewhere else."

I took a deep breath. "We always fear what we don't know. I feel like if you had a better understanding of the women—"

"What, do you think we're stupid?" someone yelled out.

"No, you're my neighbors," I said, smiling as sweetly as possible as I tried to breathe. "We're all neighbors."

"They're not *my* neighbors," someone hissed.

My heart pounded away as I prepared for the big reveal. My plan had to work. I could see my Loveladies staring up at me, believing in me, their eyes wide with hope. Even though some of them were older than me, they saw me as their mother. And as their mother, I had to protect them. I couldn't let them down. In the corner of my eye, I could see Jeff edging in on Tom. At six two, Jeff was an imposing but calm presence. Not now. Jeff looked ready to pummel Tom—or at least knock off his sunglasses.

Dear God, help me.

"What if I told you that there are a number of Loveladies in this room? Right now?"

The neighbors scanned the room. I saw one of the attendees elbow Shay, as if they were old friends commiserating, searching for the "bad" women.

"Would my Loveladies stand up?"

The only sound was the screeching of aluminum folding chair legs against linoleum as the Loveladies hesitantly stood. I watched them and smiled. They looked so prim and proper in their Sunday best. They looked better than most of the people in attendance.

I watched Shay as she nodded her head at the man who had nudged her a few seconds ago. "Lovelady, baby," she said.

Time froze as I waited for the applause or the hugs or the "wow, they're just like us" comments. My heart pounded with anticipation; this was going to be a wonderful moment.

And then…

There was more screeching of chair legs against linoleum as the neighbors pushed their seats far away from the standing women.

My heart pounded harder. My plan wasn't working. I continued speaking, hoping no one would notice that my voice was shaking.

"See, would you have picked them out before they stood up?"

"These are prisoners," someone yelled. "We don't know what they did to get into prison and we don't want to know. Now they're taking over our neighborhood and committing crimes."

These neighbors were more furious than when they had arrived. I never expected this reaction. My plan had backfired. The neighbors felt tricked.

"We don't want them here."

"Go away!"

I took a big breath to gather my composure, and for once in my life I was speechless. I stared out at the crowd, opened my mouth, but could not speak.

"You're crazy," someone yelled at me.

Quincey cleared her throat. I looked over at my girl who had gone through eight anger management classes and seemed to have finally conquered her temper. But this could reduce even the biggest pacifist to a murderer. She stood, wide-eyed, clutching her umbrella. "The only difference between you and the Loveladies," she said, "is we got caught and you didn't. Other than that, we are all the same. We're not here to hurt anybody."

"Get that crazy b**** out of here," Tom said, pointing to me.

Quincey held her umbrella in the air and narrowed her eyes at Tom. "Be careful or I'll beat your ankles with my umbrella!"

"Get her out of here. Get them all out of here!"

The Loveladies started taking off their high heels, a sign they were ready to fight.

"Calm down," I called out. "Everything will be all right."

I felt dizzy as the neighbors screamed and the Loveladies prepared to fight. How could something so good go so wrong? How could these neighbors not get it? I knew many of them, and they were good people. Didn't they understand that people were going to get out of prison no matter what? Wouldn't it be better to give them help so they didn't commit crimes again? Why couldn't they see this?

Policemen moved between Jeff and Tom, who were in each other's faces, ready to fight. They escorted Jeff up to the front of the room. One cop walked up to me and very politely said, "It might be better if you left now, Ms. Lovelady."

I glanced around at the crowd that had turned into a mob. I nodded my head.

In a blur the meeting was over. The police escorted the Loveladies and me out of the building.

I didn't know what to say. I hadn't prepared anyone for this scenario. I was so certain that the neighbors would see what I saw in these women.

Quincey hugged me. "We are a family, and we will do whatever you want us to do. We're with you."

I looked at Quincey, who was poised and calm. I had just one question for her: "Why did you tell Tom you'd beat his ankles with an umbrella?"

Quincey wiped her tears and grinned at me. "Because anything from the waist down is just a misdemeanor. They can't do anything about it if I break his ankles!"

I smiled at Quincey as we headed out of the building and into the unknown.

26

The Ice Cream Standoff

Success is not final, failure is not fatal:
It is the courage to continue that counts.

Winston Churchill

The Lovelady Whole Way House was finished. I couldn't look the women in the eyes. Their unasked questions loomed in the air, dark and heavy, like clouds before a storm. I pretended I didn't feel their weight. I pretended everything was just fine.

Melinda moved several women into her home. Jeff and I moved some of the women into the rental houses we owned. We still had twenty women living at Hob Hill, including Charmain, who refused to leave. She seemed convinced that she had somehow become my daughter and so all this zoning nonsense didn't apply to her. But like it or not, she and the other women had to be placed in some kind of housing within the next few weeks, before we hit the city's deadline.

For now, we were in limbo. I know the women believed I had some kind of plan.

I had nothing.

I was surrounded by a jumble of emotions. The women were devastated and frightened. My sons and Miranda were excited that I'd be just Mom again. Jeff, who was in Gulf Shores, was ecstatic that this ministry thing of mine had run its course. My old friends were relieved. They seemed to think I had finally seen the "error of my ways." I had been selling them on this whole "save the world" thing, and now that it had failed, perhaps I could be that jet-setting, mink-wearing, fun-loving woman they had known and loved.

They didn't say it in those exact words, but that's what they implied when I spoke to them about this latest plight. They nodded their heads and pursed their lips as if they had known it was just a matter of time before this nonsense ended. I didn't tell them that even though my house plan had been cratered, I could never resurrect the woman they had known. I also knew they could no longer be my good friends. I didn't have much in common with them.

My real friends were the Loveladies. I had grown to love them so much.

I kept this to myself because no one would understand.

A few months earlier, *I* wouldn't have understood.

I was so tired of fighting. I started to feel that if God had really wanted me to do this, He would have made it a little easier. I couldn't go back to my old ways, but I didn't need this stress anymore. I could retire to Gulf Shores, satisfied that I had tried to make a difference.

I was done.

I sat in my chair in the library and imagined lounging on a white sandy beach. I smiled, feeling all that anger, despair, and frustration slowly dissolve.

"Can we get ice cream?" Hunter asked, interrupting my daydream.

I opened my eyes. A cluster of Loveladies gathered behind Hunter, eagerly waiting for my answer. As usual, Hunter was the official Lovelady spokesperson. I laughed. Ice cream seemed like the perfect distraction.

"Sure, why not? Shannon, you take the orders and we'll go."

Shannon, one of the Loveladies, took down the ice cream orders. Then she and Hunter raced me to the car.

"We'll be right back," I called to the others.

The three of us were laughing as we drove off.

I started down the long drive and nearly crashed into a car.

It was *him.* Tom, the neighbor, barreled up our shared road at the same time I was driving down.

I'll admit that it would have been very easy for me to back up my car just a few feet and let him pass. But I didn't do that. I chose to be a different person—a person that God would not be pleased with. I glared at Tom, my heart hammering and my face hot with fury. I wanted to stomp on the accelerator and plow into him. Instead, I slammed on the brake.

Let him pull over for me. I am not budging.

In my mind, Tom was the reason the Lovelady plan was in ashes. He incited the neighbors, he passed around the petition, he stalked me in stores, and, it was rumored, he had chartered a bus to make sure as many people as possible attended the neighborhood association meeting. He was the one who had sucked out all the hope from my women who had been trying to get their lives back.

Tom returned my gaze. All I saw was the face that had killed my dreams and hopes. It was a face I hated. It was a face that filled me with a blind rage I didn't even know existed within me. My anger, frustration, and despair had not at all evaporated. They had just been on a low flame, quietly simmering. Now they were boiling over.

Tom smirked at me. That was it. I couldn't see. I couldn't think. My head felt like it was about to explode. I bolted out of my car and charged toward his.

"You're nothing but a yellow-bellied coward," I screamed in a voice I didn't recognize.

He stared at me and smiled but didn't speak. I looked back. Shannon was outside the car, holding Hunter in her arms. They looked terrified.

My God, who have I become?

"Get out of your car and talk to me," I screamed.

Shannon raced over to me and handed me my cell phone. She had called Melinda, who wanted to talk. I angrily grabbed the phone. "What?"

"Mama, get in your car and back it up the driveway," Melinda ordered.

"I will run over his ass before I move my car. I have had it with him."

I turned my head. The Loveladies were standing on the hill looking down at us, their faces filled with a mix of shock, fear, and disbelief. They were seeing a Brenda they didn't know. I had preached patience and forgiveness and advised them to turn the other cheek. I was displaying the kind of rage they had experienced in their lives.

It was the type of rage some of them had spent their lives running away from. It was the type of rage that had sent some of them to prison.

It was the kind of rage they had struggled to eliminate from their lives when they had entered my calm, God-filled home.

Out of the corner of my eye, I caught Quincey staring at me in horror. I had become a role model to her—she watched everything I did and tried to imitate me. After months of working with her, I had helped Quincey finally control her temper. For so long, she had refused to acknowledge she even had a problem, even though it was her anger that landed her in prison. She had thought it was our problem, not hers. She had blamed those around her for making her angry. But the Loveladies had shown her how ugly she could be to the other women when she lost control of her temper. And finally she had said, "I can't keep living like that."

And now I was letting her down.

I was a complete hypocrite.

I was furious for being furious.

Then I locked eyes with Carol, Tom's wife, who was standing on the other side of the road. She looked frightened. She seemed to be silently pleading with me to be reasonable.

"Do you have any idea what kind of fool you are for living with him?" I asked her. "I will run him over."

"Brenda, please stop. You don't know who you're messing with," she said.

"I don't care."

Shannon handed me the phone again. Jeff was on the line.

"Brenda," he said, in a calm, measured tone, "you should—"

"Just go buy some property," I hissed at him. "You know you're happy this isn't working. You don't care." He tried to speak, but I clicked the phone off.

I stormed back to my car and sat...and sat...and sat...for at least an hour and a half. I was not budging. Tom was not budging. His wife stood by his car, pleading with him to move. My cell phone kept ringing, but I ignored the calls from Melinda, Jeff, Beau, and Matthew.

Police sirens blared. Soon the road was jammed with cop cars. I have no idea who called the police, but they couldn't do anything anyway. They ran our names in the system to see if either of us had any outstanding warrants or anything that could get us arrested. Neither of us did. They shook their heads and told us we were being ridiculous. They seemed to be staring at me when they said this.

"You don't have far to back up," they pleaded with me. "Why don't you just move your car a few feet and call it a night?"

I shook my head no, just like a stubborn child. I was not moving for anyone, even the police. I would stay there forever if I had to.

"I told y'all she's crazy," Tom yelled from his car.

I sat and sat and sat.

Later—I'm not sure how much time had passed—Melinda arrived. She parked her car behind Tom's and walked up the hill toward me. She opened my car door and grabbed my arm.

"Mother, what are you doing? I've never seen you like this," she whispered.

"Get used to it," I hissed.

"Mother, please," Melinda begged, her eyes wet with tears. She gently tugged on my arm; I slowly got out of the car. I'm not sure why I moved for her when I wouldn't budge for anyone, even the police. Maybe it was that look of sadness in those beautiful blue eyes—the same look I'd seen a lifetime ago when we'd been accused of fraud by those horrible IRS agents. I had hated those monsters for causing my daughter such pain. Now *I* was the monster.

Melinda didn't say a word as she got in the driver's seat and backed my car a few small feet into the driveway.

And with that, the great Ice Cream Standoff was over.

I have reflected on that night more times than you can imagine. It has haunted my dreams and my waking hours. When I started the program, I thought it was because I wanted to help those "unfortunate, troubled" women. That night, I realized with shock that I needed them more than they ever needed me.

I needed them desperately. These women were going to make it. But I was terrified I couldn't make it without them.

Psychiatrists talk about "now moments," short periods of time in our life during which something so important happens that it changes our future. They are moments that become dividing lines in our life. Once the line is crossed, nothing is ever the same again.

Despite what I had told myself, I knew as I sat stubbornly in my car that I wasn't done with the Loveladies. I didn't want to live an empty, unfulfilled life. I didn't want to wander aimlessly, wasting time like I had for so many years. God had shown me my destiny, and I didn't want to lose it. I wanted to change lives.

I would find a way.

I just needed a different plan.

27

Eating an Elephant

Miracles are a retelling in small letters of the very same story which is written across the whole world in letters too large for some of us to see.

C. S. Lewis

It was just like any other Sunday drive, except instead of touring the beautiful countryside, I was driving Jeff into a wreck of a neighborhood in downtown Birmingham. Melinda was following us in her car.

I had explained to Jeff that despite the obstacles, I didn't want to give up on the Loveladies. I told him that I could keep the whole-way house dream alive.

I had rehearsed my speech.

"We have changed lives. I don't want to stop now. I do not believe God is ready to close down this ministry yet. I believe He is not through with it...or us."

Jeff nodded his head. "Mmm-hmm."

Was he even listening?

I parked in front of the boarded-up medical center that I had stumbled upon a few days earlier. I had been driving around Lakewood, a less desirable area of the city, searching for buildings with For Sale signs on them. I had found a small office building that would house about forty women. I kept searching for other buildings but always wound around to the front of that same office building.

I stopped and called the number on the sign. A man answered the phone and told me I could get the key for the building at the boarded-up old hospital across the street. He told me to keep banging on the door until the security guard answered, and he would give me the key.

I banged on the door and finally an old man answered. As he searched for the key, I walked into the old hospital.

Immediately I knew.

This was it. This old hospital was exactly what we needed not only to keep the dream alive but to take the dream out of its infancy and into maturity. It was a 280,000-square-foot, four-story behemoth that spanned an entire block.

Inside, the rooms were crumbling, filled with debris, alive with vermin. But I saw its future glory—bedrooms; offices; rooms for teaching, counseling, and worship; a day-care center. I even envisioned a puppet theater where the children of the women could perform and be entertained.

The man handed me the key to the office building across the street, but I was no longer interested in it. This vacant old hospital was the Lovelady Center. My heart pounded as chills raced through my body.

And now I was back showing the facility to Jeff.

As we stepped out of the car, Jeff surveyed the area and Melinda joined us.

"So where is it?"

This is a mistake, I thought. I should have eased him in to this. I was feeding Jeff the whole elephant instead of giving him baby bites. To make matters worse, as I stood there my vision vanished. All I could see was what they could see—a dilapidated hospital. Where was that beautiful, thriving center I had envisioned? It was gone.

I have learned that when fear overtakes you, you cannot hear or see God. It's just like when Peter tried to walk on water. He did great until he became afraid and took his eyes off Jesus.

And then...*splash.*

I took a deep breath and pointed to the hospital right in front of us.

"This is the Lovelady Center," I announced as if it had already happened.

Jeff looked at me to see if I was joking. When he realized I wasn't, I thought he might have a heart attack. He stumbled backward, and his eyes nearly popped out of his skull. His mouth hung open as he looked at the building and back at me and then back at the building. He was too stunned to speak.

We stood in silence, staring at the building. I knew Jeff saw this wreck as a turning point for me, for us. This would no longer be a hobby or even a vocation. This would be my life. This would be Jeff's life too. I waited for him to yell or laugh or get in the car and drive far away.

"What...what...," he choked out. "What about our lives?"

"This is what I need to do. These women mean everything to me."

He shook his head as words failed him. He looked at the building and then back at me.

"Jeff, I have to do this."

"I thought I'd heard it all from you, but this is the craziest thing yet."

I smiled reassuringly. "It's crazy, but I know I can make it happen. And when I do, we won't be changing a few lives. We will be changing thousands of lives."

Melinda stared at me with those beautiful blue eyes. I knew she would understand. When she opened her mouth to speak, I was certain she'd offer support and encouragement.

"Mom, this is borderline insanity."

I smiled reassuringly. "I know. Isn't it wonderful? I know this is what God wants. All we have to do is believe and take the first step."

As I stood there preaching to my congregation of two, I saw that center rise up again. It was no longer the old hospital, but the beautiful Lovelady Center. As I spoke, I knew it would happen. If God could change me and all those women, why not a little ol' building?

Jeff let out a soft chuckle. He wasn't angry, and he wasn't going to laugh in my face or drive away and leave me. He sounded resigned to the fact that I had made up my mind and somehow I would make this happen. "You know, you'll need a miracle to pull this off."

I smiled at him and nodded.

The miracle was about to happen.

It had already started.

Epilogue

There are only two ways to live your life.
One is as though nothing is a miracle. The other
is as though everything is a miracle.

ALBERT EINSTEIN

In 2005 the Lovelady Center opened, much to the surprise of everyone—especially me. There is never a day that I do not look around the center in wonderment. People try to give me and those around me credit for the center. But I tell them that the credit goes to God. God has accomplished this *in spite* of me and all my weaknesses.

After showing the building to Jeff and Melinda, I discovered that the abandoned hospital was available for $1.3 million—money I didn't have. But Jeff figured out a way to draft a contract that gave me the option of buying the hospital if I could come up with the money in ninety days.

We did it. It turned out FEMA needed the building to temporarily house three hundred Hurricane Katrina victims, so they asked us if they could lease the building from us. We used their money for the down payment of the building. The deals closed within thirty minutes of each other. At both closings, everyone was shaking their head and wondering what had just happened. They couldn't figure it out, but I could. A miracle.

We never knew how we would pay the bills at the center, but each month we somehow squeaked by. I had to fight the gas and power companies, who threatened to turn off the power and render my women homeless. Each month, we scraped together the mortgage.

Then one day an elderly nun took a tour of our facility. I didn't think much about it. People toured our place all the time. Everyone tried to figure out how we made it work.

"God is at work here," she told some people after her tour. By the end of the week, we were informed that we didn't need to make any more payments on the center. It turned out this nun was also the director of St. Vincent's Hospital, our hospital's parent company—and the mortgage holder of the building. Another miracle.

Since we opened, thousands of women have gone through our program, and the Lovelady Center has been recognized as the largest faith-based transitional center for women and their children in the country. The center offers psychological counseling, career counseling, drug addiction treatment, high school and college courses, worship, and prayer. At any time, there are about four hundred women as well as over one hundred of their children living in the center. We have a child-care development center, medical and dental clinics, and legal services available. There is even a beauty salon. We are like a thriving city within a city. Sometimes we have three generations staying with us—grandmother, mother, daughter. I see their lives transformed in ways no one ever thought possible.

We no longer take only former prisoners. Some women come to us as part of an alternative sentencing arrangement with the courts. Other women just get into trouble with life, not the law, and we try to help them too. Sometimes a woman will walk in off the street, and we do our best to make room for her.

There are African American women and white women. There are rich and poor women. There are Christians, Jews, agnostics, and atheists. Many atheists enter our doors determined not to be swayed by our faith. There is no challenge I love better. I explain to them that no one has to change to become a Lovelady. But somehow, most do. It simply shows the power of love through God. That is what we are called to do—give love. There is no greater gift.

We serve 1,600 meals a day—584,000 a year. Our 185 rooms are filled to capacity most nights. Parole boards from eight other states send women to us, including New York, Texas, Utah, Washington, Louisiana, Mississippi, Arkansas, and Georgia. Our operating budget for the Lovelady Center is $3.5 million a year, which we raise from donors, foundations, and state and local resources. We also generate about $1.5 million annually from our 30,000-square-foot thrift shop, which employs fifty women—all of them former Loveladies. When a woman gets to a certain level in the program, she pays $30 a week for day care and $130 a week for room, board, and program fees.

I've been approached by city officials throughout the country who want me to help them duplicate our program. Even government officials from Romania toured the center and asked me to visit their country to help implement a program there. I declined, but they have kept in touch and recently informed me that they opened the Butterfly Program for Women, which focuses on rehabilitating survivors of human trafficking.

The need is much greater than I could have imagined. Would I ever have started down this path had I known? Of course, I would love to answer with a resounding *yes!* But that's not true. I believe God gives us small steps of faith to take one at a time. Martin Luther King Jr. said we do not wait to see the entire staircase before climbing. Such is our walk with God. We climb those stairs, and one day we realize we've climbed higher than we ever imagined. At least that is how it has been for me.

These women come to the center all wanting the same things—love and hope. When these women enter Lovelady, they've been so crushed by life and so stripped of hope. They don't even know hope exists. If you peel down what the center does, it is very simple: we show these women the possibilities. They never even knew they had any.

And the first person they meet when they walk through the Lovelady doors? One of my best friends—a soft-hearted woman with a belly laugh and a great sense of humor who can whip up the best seafood gumbo in all of Alabama.

Shay.

Shay, the woman who years ago was so angry, so mean, so scary that when she arrived at my front door, the women I had hired all ran out on me. Now *she* welcomes the women and introduces them to *me.*

Shay greets our new residents—women just as scared and angry as she was—and tells them her story. And her words reassure them that with hope, anything is possible.

Where They Are Now

The Loveladies

Today, Shay is director of intake operations at the Lovelady Center. She has reunited with her sister and oldest daughter, although she still has a strained relationship with her youngest daughter.

"She can't get past the past. I tell her I'm not that person anymore. I tell her she's boxing with ghosts and that my door is always open. I tell her it's too bad she doesn't want me in her life because she's missing out on something great. I don't try to fight that battle with her, but when she's ready, I'm always here, waiting."

Today the only thing Shay is addicted to is Walmart. She's there almost every day. A few weeks ago, she came back from a shopping excursion and was in tears. "Some man bumped into my cart," she explained. "I turned around and almost snapped at him. And you know what he said? 'I'm sorry, ma'am.' He called *me* ma'am! I never imagined a world where someone would call me ma'am!"

Shay has had some health problems as a result of her years on the street. But she never misses a day of work. She loves being at the center and helping these women. I cannot imagine my life without having known her. Shay and I go on speaking engagements, and we have so much fun telling our story. She is one of the most influential people in my life.

"Never in my wildest dreams did I imagine this life," Shay says. "I have a home. I have insurance. I can go to the doctor. People don't know how important that is. Once, I didn't care if I was healthy or not. Now I do, and so do a lot of other people. I am so blessed. I respect people and they respect me. I have a job that I love. I have people who love me unconditionally. That's rags to riches, baby. Rags to riches."

TIFFANY still cleans my house but also works as a receptionist at the center. She lives in an apartment—that nice, neat place of her own she always wanted. She spends all her free time cleaning while singing to Mary J. Blige. "I love cleaning—it relaxes me," she says. "I still love my OdoBan and bleach. My place looks like a mini Brenda house."

Tiffany has a good relationship with her two older daughters, now in their twenties. "We talk all the time." She hopes to become closer to her teenage daughter.

True to her word, Tiffany has not touched drugs since December 26, 2004. "I never will. I'm too happy with my life." But despite all of my budgeting classes, spending money is Tiffany's major vice. She will spend her money on anything.

Tiffany is the center's unofficial social director and keeps in touch with Loveladies past and present. Everyone knows Suga-Suga, and everyone loves her.

QUINCEY, my once snapping turtle, is a hotel manager at a major hotel chain. She is so popular with the guests that they specifically ask for her to handle their reservations and requests. No one would ever guess that this sweet, friendly, happy woman ever had an anger problem. "I love the new me. I love what I do. I love that I can control my temper," she says. "I'm not going to lie—I still get mad. I'm only human. But I don't get so angry that I go to that other level. I breathe and count to ten before I speak."

She says there isn't a day that goes by that she doesn't think about her victim. "I am responsible for ending someone's life. But I know God has forgiven me and I have finally forgiven myself."

At first, the future didn't seem too promising for CHARMAIN. Even after all the women had moved out of Hob Hill, Charmain would not leave. When I told her it was time to spread her wings, she was angry with me and acted as if I were abandoning her. She had convinced herself that I was her mother, and she felt that by forcing her to move out, I had betrayed her. She moved in with family and started selling dope again. She served another four years in Tutwiler for distribution. When she was released, she came to the center and said, "I don't want to live like this anymore. I'm tired of this life. I want to work hard and make money, but I don't want to break the law. I want to live right."

When I asked why she was so angry with me when she had to move out, she said, "I didn't want to let that love go. I thought once I left, it was gone for good. I didn't realize it was something permanent. I understand that now."

Charmain graduated from the program. She now works as a housekeeper at a local hotel and also does part-time maintenance at the center. She's developed a close relationship with her son, who is a star college football player.

A few years ago, TERRY called me and asked if she could come home. I said, "Of course." She didn't have anything—not even a purse with a wallet and identification. She had to start all over again. But she made it through the program and graduated. She works as a nanny, as well as in day care at the center. She loves being with children and is wonderful with the kids.

"My mom and I have a good relationship now. We're closer than we've been and she's really helping me get my life together," she says. Terry remembers the day when she was arrested at my house as being a low point in her life.

"I wasn't done using. Back then, I wasn't ready to get clean and didn't want to even try. Now I wake up every day trying to live a good, clean life. I don't ever want to go back."

Annette works in maintenance at the center and is looking to move into an apartment. She has a strong relationship with her family and talks to her parents almost every day.

After all these years, she has a confession. "I did put those ants in Shay's bed, but don't tell Shay." After all, Shay and Annette have become really good friends. "I hated that woman, but now I love her like a sister," Annette says.

Melissa is a hairstylist. She hasn't touched drugs in fourteen years, although a few years ago she had some problems with alcohol and came back to the center, went through the program, and graduated. She keeps in touch with the women and still has all the clothes, shoes, and purses she took when I cleaned out my closets. "I must have moved one hundred times since those days, but I'm still living off my Lovelady clothes. I love my real cowhide purse."

Suzanne left Hob Hill and her prison days behind and has never looked back. She is now a registered nurse in Birmingham. Her name has been changed for this book. She wants to keep her former life private, but she keeps in touch with some of the Loveladies, who report that she is happy and healthy and still addicted to her cell phone.

One day a few years ago, I was walking down the Lovelady hallway when I saw a familiar face. It was Parthina.

"Oh, did you have a nice Thanksgiving?" I asked her, even though it had been seven years since she disappeared from my house.

Her reply? "It was good."

"Well, I'm glad you enjoyed it," I said as I kept walking down the hall. I think she wanted some reaction from me. I think she felt a bit of satisfaction that she made history by being the first Lovelady to leave the program. I wouldn't give it to her.

Later she talked about that time: "When I went home for Thanksgiving I went back to my old habits with my old friends. Then I lived in and out of motels. When I sobered up, I couldn't believe what I had given up for this life. A few years later, I was ready to be clean. I called Shay at the center. I told her I was ready to be clean. She drove right over and took me back to the center."

Parthina stuck with the program and graduated. She's living and working various jobs in Birmingham.

The Employee Who Became a Lovelady

In August 2007, Melinda burst into my office, her eyes as big as saucers. "Mother, a judge in Florida wants to send a woman to us."

"Fine," I said. "Send her over."

"Mom...it's Stephanie."

She explained that Stephanie had been arrested in Florida for allegedly stealing money from an employer. "No way," I replied. "I don't want anything to do with that woman."

That night I fell right to sleep, but I woke up, tossing and turning. All I could think about were the Loveladies to whom I had preached forgiveness. I had asked women like Tiffany and Shay to forgive their abusers—people who had done such horrible things to them. I had explained to all the Loveladies the meaning of the Lord's Prayer. If we don't forgive, how can we ask for forgiveness?

Here I was, Brenda Spahn, a supposedly changed, loving, and forgiving woman. I wrestled with this all night. I didn't want to see this woman ever again, yet how could I not practice what I preached? I was being a hypocrite. The words of the Bible echoed in my head. *We have to let Jesus be the perfect example of who we are supposed to be.*

I knew what I had to do, but I didn't want to do it.

The next morning I called the judge. "I made a hasty decision, but I was wrong. Please send Stephanie to me."

When she arrived, I told Stephanie, "Don't look at me. Don't talk to me. Just go through the program and get out of here. I don't want to see you at all."

Three days later, I had forgiven her. I had spent those days praying. I had also spent those days talking to Stephanie. (I had told her to stay away but kept calling her into my office to hear her story!) Ultimately, I understood why she did what she did.

Sometimes it takes a while to learn all those things you teach—like forgiveness and hope. Sometimes you have to remember that it applies to you too.

So STEPHANIE graduated from the program, worked at various positions in the center, and is now the director of development. She was one of the first to make me realize that people cannot change simply because we give them love, buy them clothes, and fix their hair. They have to truly desire a new way of life with their entire being.

When I met Stephanie, I wanted a new life for her much more than she wanted one for herself.

This time around, she was ready. And today she's flourishing.

My Family

MELINDA is the director of the Lovelady Center. She oversees all programs and the sixty-member staff. Occasionally my input is necessary, but I find that the need is decreasing—the center is in good hands. In the rare instances when Melinda needs my help, I feel needed, which makes me feel good. However, my sweet blue-eyed daughter now carries most of the authority. It won't be long until she will be completely filling my shoes. To be honest, she will be better than I was. Melinda has a passion that burns long into the night while I am asleep.

Melinda is also the fastest texter you can imagine. I decided I was going to set up my phone to do group text messages so I could be just like Melinda. I set up the groups in four, with one being my immediate family and closest friends. I sent a text out to my "family group," telling them how much I loved them. But I did something wrong. Somehow the whole town, even the city council and the mayor, received my text.

I was so embarrassed. It taught me a lesson: leave the technical things to Melinda. Leave most things to Melinda.

This is probably one of the reasons Melinda tells everyone that *I* am her full-time job and the center is only a part-time gig.

When the women first arrived at the house, MIRANDA, then a teenager, kept her distance. Now she is as involved as any of us. She oversees the Lovelady's child-care center.

She and her husband, Rieder, have seven children. Three of them are adopted. She's the most amazing mother I have ever seen. Some people have a gift with children. Miranda is one of those people. She loves them all—her own and the Lovelady children.

BEAU originally moved to Gulf Shores to work on our beach property. Who would've ever guessed that after the storm and the economic meltdown, we would no longer own beach property? Beau loves the beach and is a very gifted builder, so he stayed there to build houses. We kind of joke sadly that Beau seems to run from God's will. Since Beau was a small child, he has felt called to the ministry, but he refuses to go.

Sounds like someone else, doesn't it?

Now that thousands of Loveladies have gone through the program, my children—especially Beau—have accepted the fact that they are not the only ones who call me Mama.

"It used to infuriate me," says Beau. "I'd tell them, 'That is not your mama; that's my mama.' But I understand now that a lot of these girls never had a mama and that's what they're longing for. I finally came to peace with it."

At six five, MATTHEW is a gentle giant, an entrepreneur in the real estate business. He and his wife, Rebekah, have three children. Matthew is dedicated to the center and is on the board.

HUNTER is now a teenager. Since he was there from the beginning, Hunter feels as if he is in charge of the center—and he is there almost every day. He argues nearly every day with Suga-Suga and Shay. They were all raised together, so they act more like siblings than adult and child. Hunter is ready to take over the world, but first he has to get through high school.

The Scriptures say there will be trials. I wish I could say things have been easy for JEFF and me in this great adventure. A few years ago when the real estate market collapsed, Gulf Shores was hit particularly hard. The whole area was riddled with foreclosure signs. Jeff hung on as long as he could, but eventually we filed for bankruptcy—something I had been determined never to do again.

Jeff was devastated. His credit, his reputation, and his assets were his world before he met me. He prided himself on his great credit and his ability to make money. He signed on to marry a businesswoman, travel the world, retire early, and grow old together in some beautiful place. Instead, he found himself bankrupt and married to a woman crazy enough to open her home to ex-cons. This was not the life he had ever imagined. If you would have told me he'd go through all this and still stand by me, I never would have believed it.

Jeff didn't want to work in the center, but he can't seem to keep his hands out of things. He'd hear me on the phone fighting with officials or see the work that needed to be done. Slowly he became involved. He began saying, "Let me handle this. Let me handle that."

When we moved into the hospital, Jeff's real estate expertise was a huge asset. He helped get the building up to code. He hired people for all the construction work and all major repairs. He budgeted the money for us. Over time I realized, or I should say I helped him realize, or rather, God helped him realize, that we really need his help to run the place. He fills a tremendous void—even though he complains the whole time. But I know he believes he is where God wants him to be.

Jeff is now director of building operations.

I, BRENDA LOVELADY SPAHN, am executive director of the Lovelady Center. During the last few years I have fought many battles—with the city, with bill collectors, with the center's neighbors, with business associations. I have been front-page news many times. After one particularly nasty article, I locked myself in my room and stuffed myself with peanut butter and jelly sandwiches until I was almost sick.

Butterball had returned. I decided there and then I would never go to work again.

The next morning I got up and went to work like it had never happened.

I believe God takes us through different kinds of fire in our lives to see exactly what we are made of. It's like the Lord is a blacksmith. He tempers us like we are steel. He puts us through hot fire, hits us with His hammer, and dumps us in ice-cold water. If we make it through that process, we pass the test. Tempered steel is so much more valuable.

I face every test that comes my way. I never ask "Why me?" anymore. I used to do that all the time. I once thought I had problems. But I have seen so much heartache in the lives of the women sent to me. I have seen so many horrible things that I can no longer think the way I used to. You know the old saying, "I thought I had it bad because I did not have any shoes until I met the man with no feet"?

Well, I have met that man. In my case, it was hundreds of women.

The Scriptures teach us that we must die to find ourselves. That is what I have done. The old is gone and the new is here.

I like the new Brenda much more. I truly feel like the most blessed person in the world because of my faith, because God called me to do this. I see what God can do in our lives, in women's lives. He changes them, He changes us, and it's just amazing.

I used to love traveling and exploring beautiful places—the Greek isles, the Caribbean Sea—and I could stare at my gorgeous Gulf Shores vistas for hours. But nothing is more beautiful than a face illuminated by that first spark of hope.

People say I'm such a wonderful person for doing what I do. But they don't understand that I'm the lucky one. There's something so incredible about looking into the faces of women who are devoid of hope and watching their expressions change when they discover they have a future and it's going to be great.

I have been fortunate to be able to provide that spark in their lives.

But it's God who ignites the flame.

Acknowledgments

In the beginning there were people who played an instrumental role in helping us, who deserve acknowledgment for their perseverance and belief in what God was doing: the Lovelady staff, Don and Susie Ankenbrandt, Kim and Sue Ratliff, Greg and Ann Giles, Dean and Ron Giles, Joe Medina, John and Beverly McNeil, Annie Meeks, the Honorable John Amari, Ken Garner, Foster Cook and UAB TASC, Special Forces for Jesus, Michael and Lisa French with Advocate Ministries, Bill and Joyce French with Advocate Ministries, Don McGriff and the State Board of Pardons and Paroles, and Sister Dinah White and St. Vincent's Hospital.

I have always dreamed of writing a book about the Loveladies. The following people turned that dream into a reality: Farley Chase; and the WaterBrook Multnomah team, including Ken Petersen, Steve Cobb, Heather Brown, Carrie Freimuth, Mark Ford, Beverly Rykerd, Ashley Boyer, Kendall Davis, Lori Addicott, Laura Wright, Julia Wallace, and Terri Schurz.

The Lovelady Center is the largest and most successful nonprofit transitional center for women in the country. It services 450 women and children every day, providing substance abuse counseling, drug rehabilitation, meals, childcare, career counseling, job training, job placement, and continued education courses to women working to establish sucessful lives outside of prison walls.

To learn more about The Lovelady Center or how you can help, visit www.LoveladyCenter.org.